D1383536

Hudson Valley Voyage

An Exploration of Four Seasons and Four Centuries

The Hudson River begins its 315-mile seaward voyage at Lake Tear of the Clouds in the Adirondacks, swirling down the flanks of Mount Marcy (left). The Hudson is young. Its current riverbed was carved just 12,000 years ago, as the last glaciers retreated.

The river flows past Vanderbilt Mansion National Historic Site in Hyde Park (overleaf), and the United States Military Academy at West Point (ensuing pages), 50 miles north of its entry into the Atlantic Ocean at New York City.

1

Mohonk Mountain House has been a four-season destination for nature-bound pilgrims since 1869. This National Historic Landmark (above and right), one of America's last great Victorian resort hotels, encompasses 2,200 acres astride the Shawangunk Mountains.

Hudson Valley Voyage

Through the Seasons,
Through the Years

Photographs by Ted Spiegel
Text by Reed Sparling

Involvement Media, Inc.

Dedication

From Ted Spiegel:

To my grandchildren –
    Olivia, Samuel, and Scott

From Reed Sparling:

In memory of Leon Sparling –
    father, friend, teacher

Library of Congress Control Number:
2007903836

ISBN 978-1-929373-16-1

Copyright © 2007 Involvement Media, Incorporated

Photographs © 2007 Ted Spiegel

Text © 2007 Reed Sparling

Published by Involvement Media, Incorporated

P.O. Box 444, Fishkill, NY 12524

Project editor: Reed Sparling

Art director: Marc Tolen

Cartography: Matthew Bazylewskyj

**All rights reserved. No part of the contents
of this book may be reproduced without the
written permission of the publisher.**

**Color prepress by National Geographic Society
Digital Imaging Services, Washington, D.C.**

Printing by Graphic Research Unlimited, Fanwood, NJ

Hudson Valley Voyage **is available at special
discounts for bulk purchase by corporations,
institutions, and other organizations.**

For more information:

Web: hudsonvalleyvoyage.com

eMail: info@hudsonvalleyvoyage.com

Phone: 1-888-EYE-HAND (1-888-393-4263)

Historic encounters abound throughout the Hudson Valley. The seven stone houses in the National Historic Landmark District on New Paltz's Huguenot Street date back as far as 1705. Reenacting a Revolutionary War naval engagement in the Hudson Highlands, Poughkeepsie's sloop *Clearwater* (at far right) engages the replica brig *Providence*.

Table of Contents

Hudson Valley Voyage

17th Century: Exploration

14 The voyage begins: Henry Hudson sets sail

16 The beaver: New Netherland's four-legged gold mine

18 The purchase of Manhattan Island

20 A novel way of colonizing: The patroon system

22 Securing peace with Native Americans

24 Everyday life

26 The Dutch surrender to the British without a fight

28 Preserving our 17th-century heritage

30 Winter

18th Century: Revolution

42 Down on the farm: An agricultural Eden

44 Natural resourcefulness: Tapping the valley's bounty

46 Rumblings of rebellion

48 Benedict Arnold's triumph and treachery

50 The storming of Stony Point

52 General Washington quashes a coup

54 Alexander Hamilton "sells" the constitution

56 President Washington commands the nation

58 Spring

19th Century: Innovation

76 Robert Fulton steams up the Hudson

78 Establishing America's military academy

80 The world's "Eighth Wonder" – The Erie Canal

82 Rent-paying farmers go on the warpath

84 Creating the Romantic landscape

86 Old tales, new voices:
The making of American literature

88 Slavery's Underground Railroad
chugs through the valley

90 Forging an industrial powerhouse
along the Hudson

92 Nature nurtured: Winning the battle for the
Catskills, the Adirondacks, and the Palisades

20th Century: Preservation

108 Immigrants enter through Ellis Island

110 Franklin D. Roosevelt's valley legacies

112 Eleanor Roosevelt: Human rights champion

114 Abstract Expressionism:
New York's art movement

116 Standing up for the environment

118 Ever upward: The materials behind
Manhattan's building boom

120 Reaching for the sky: Steeples and spires

122 Centuries of sacrifice:
The Hudson Valley remembers

124 The Hudson River Valley National Heritage Area

An Exploration of Four Seasons and Four Centuries

94 Summer

Guide to the Hudson Valley

126 Hudson history time line

131 An invitation from Reed Sparling

135 Hudson Valley maps

140 Historic sites and their Web sites

144 Fall

Overleaf: Two seasons at Popolopen Gorge, within the Palisades Interstate Park's 100,000 acres.

Henry Hudson's contract with the Dutch East India Company for a voyage of discovery (1609)

On this eighth of January, in the year of our Lord one thousand six hundred and nine, the Directors of the East India Company of the Chamber of Amsterdam…and Master Henry Hudson, Englishman…have agreed in manner following, to wit: That the said Directors shall in the first place equip a small vessel or yacht of about thirty lasts [60 tons] burden, well provided with men, provisions and other necessaries, with which the above named Hudson shall, about the first of April, sail in order to search for a passage by the north, around the north side of Nova Zembla, and shall continue thus along that parallel until he shall be able to sail southward to the latitude of sixty degrees. He shall obtain as much knowledge of the lands as can be done without any considerable loss of time, and if it is possible return immediately in order to make a faithful report and relation of his voyage to the Directors, and to deliver over his journals, log-books, and charts, together with an account of everything whatsoever which shall happen to him during the voyage without keeping anything back.

The 17th Century

"The land is the finest for cultivation that I ever in my life set foot upon."

Thanks to an English mariner, the Dutch struck it rich in the sweepstakes for North America's treasures.

Henry Hudson's birth date and birthplace are unknown. His first entry in the annals of exploration occurred in 1607. That's when the Muscovy Company, a British firm that bankrolled voyages of discovery, hired Hudson to command a ship in search of the fabled Northwest Passage, a direct water route from Europe to the riches of the Orient. Heading due north, Hudson and his 12-man crew endured frozen seas, rotting food supplies, even a whale attack, eventually coming within 600 miles of the North Pole. Unbelievably, they lived to tell their audacious tale.

A shortcut to Asia was Hudson's Holy Grail, and he wasted little time mounting another expedition, again for the Muscovy Company, in 1608. The following year, he found an employer with even deeper pockets – the Dutch East India Company. The first multinational corporation, it was a major force in Europe's profit-driven globalization, accounting for 60 percent of the world's shipping. But the company lusted for even greater dominance over the English, Spanish, French, and Portuguese fleets. All traders relied on a southern route to the Orient; the Dutch hired Hudson to find a faster, northern course.

Hudson and his crew – probably a dozen or more men; all that's certain is that two other English seamen were aboard – left Amsterdam on the 85-foot *Half Moon* on April 4, 1609. Per his contract, Hudson sailed in a northeasterly direction until encountering pack ice around Novaya Zemlya, Russian islands in the Arctic Ocean. Instead of returning to port, he headed west, toward North America, then south, searching for a route straight through the continent. The ship ventured as far as Cape Henry, close to the Jamestown settlement in Virginia established in 1607 by Hudson's seafaring pal John Smith, before backtracking to the mouth of the river now bearing his name.

Detail of WPA mural, Rhinebeck Post Office. Left: Replica ship *Half Moon*.

On September 12, 1609, the tri-masted *Half Moon* began its three-week journey into a land fresh to European eyes – past the towering Palisades, through the craggy Hudson Highlands, within the shadow of the Catskills. The men ventured just beyond present-day Albany, where the water was deemed too shallow to proceed further. All along their route they encountered Native Americans. Some meetings were peaceful; others resulted in the death of crewmen or Indians.

Any disappointment at Hudson's failure to locate a speedier route to Asia was quickly forgotten once his employers discovered that this "pleasant land," as first mate Robert Juet described it, held its own riches – animal furs. The company wasted no time claiming the territory and profiting from it. One Dutch merchant ship returned to the river's shores in 1610. Another five arrived in 1613, bearing traders who established Fort Nassau, near Albany.

The following year, Dutch cartographers drew the first chart on which the land around Henry Hudson's "River of Mountains," as he called it, was dubbed "New Netherland." The colony was literally on the map.

Meeting the valley's native population: From Henry Hudson's journal

When I came on shore, the swarthy natives all stood and sang in their fashion. Their clothing consists of the skins of foxes and other animals, which they dress and make the garments from skins of various sorts. Their food is Turkish wheat, which they cook by baking, and it is excellent eating. They soon came on board one after another in their canoes, which are made of a single piece of wood. Their weapons are bows and arrows, pointed with sharp stones, which they fashion with hard resin... They always carry with them all their goods...

I sailed to the shore in one of their canoes, with...the chief of a tribe, consisting of forty men and seventeen women; these I saw there in a house well constructed of oak bark, and circular in shape... It contained a great quantity of maize, and beans of the last year's growth, and there lay near the house for the purpose of drying enough to load three ships, besides what was growing in the fields. On our coming near the house, two mats were spread out to sit upon, and immediately some food was served in well-made red wooden bowls; two men were also dispatched at once with bows and arrows in quest of game, who soon after brought in a pair of pigeons which they had just shot... They supposed that I would remain with them for the night, but I returned after a short time on board the ship. The land is the finest for cultivation that I ever in my life set foot upon, and it also abounds in trees of every description. The natives are a very good people; for when they saw that I would not remain, they supposed that I was afraid of their bows, and taking the arrows, they broke them in pieces, and threw them into the fire.

"Beavers not only can run wonderfully over the earth, but in the water they seem as active as fishes."

Beaver bonanza: A portrait of the precious mammal from Adriaen Van der Donck's *A Description of the New Netherlands* (1655)

The beaver's skin is rough, but very thickly set with fine wool (fur) of an ash gray color, inclining to blue… Outside of the coat of fur many shining hairs appear, which are called wind hairs, that more properly are winter hairs, for those fall out in summer and appear again in the fall. This outer coat is of a chestnut brown color – the browner the better – it sometimes will be somewhat reddish… The skins usually are first sent to Russia where they are highly esteemed for the outside shining hair… There the skins are used for mantle linings, and are also cut into strips for borders… Whoever there has the most and costliest fur trimmings is esteemed the greatest, as with us, the finest stuffs and gold and silver embroidery are considered the appendages of the great. After the hairs have fallen out, or are worn, and the peltries become old and dirty, and apparently useless, we get the articles back and convert the fur into hats, before which it cannot be well used for this purpose, for unless the beaver has been worn and is greasy and dirty, it will not felt properly… The coats which the Indians make of beaver skins, and have worn a long time around their bodies, until the same have become foul with sweat and grease – those afterwards are used by the hatters and make the best hats.

The beavers are so quick that they not only can run wonderfully over the earth… avoiding men and dogs; but in the water they seem as active as fishes. Therefore the Indians must take them in traps; or to take and kill them with long rammers (which have lances affixed at the ends) inserted at the holes of their burrows… The beavers keep in deep swamps, at the waters and morasses, where no settlements are. Still when they are beset and bitten by dogs, they can defend themselves very well, and do great injury to a common dog, when they take hold of the same with their foreteeth…

The form of a beaver resembles the shape of a cucumber which has a short stem, or a duck that has the neck and head cut off, or like a ball of yarn wound in long form and flattened a little, being often thicker than long…

From December to the first of June, the skins are good, and then they are killed. The fall skins have the winter hairs in part, with very little fur. The summer skins and those taken from ungrown beavers are of little value. Still the Indians kill all they find when they are hunting

The beaver tails are flattish, without hair, coated with a skin which appears as if set with fish scales, and when chopped up with the flesh of the beaver, it is a delicate food, and is always preserved for the Emperor's table, whenever a beaver is caught in Germany, which seldom happens. The beaver tails excel all other flesh taken on land and in the water…. The Indians will seldom part with it, unless on an extraordinary occasion as a present.

Reprinted with permission of Syracuse University Press.

When is an infestation of rodents a good thing? When the critters are beaver and there's a lofty price on their heads. The aquatic mammal *Castor canadensis* was the economic lifeblood of the burgeoning Dutch colony on the Hudson. The yearly profits from their skins to the Dutch West India Company, founded in 1621 to manage the colony's affairs, ranged between $50,000 and $100,000, depending on how successful the Indians were at trapping the bucktoothed beasts. In the 1640s alone, as many as 80,000 were killed. The pelts became the colony's currency, traded to the West Indies for sugar, Africa for slaves, and Europe for housewares.

Ulster County beaver lodge. Left: beaver at Bear Mountain Zoo.

Oddly, it was not the luxurious reddish-brown outer fur of the creatures that was prized by the Dutch, but the dull gray undercoat, which was made into a soft felt. Beaver hats, conical in shape with a wide brim, were so valued that they were handed down in families for generations. The importance of the animals to the founding of New Netherland was reflected in the naming of the Dutch settlement near present-day Albany, site of the colony's prime trading post. It was dubbed Beverwyck – beaver town. In a more lasting tribute, a likeness of the animal still adorns Albany's official seal.

Hunted nearly to extinction by 1660, the beaver made a grand comeback once it was no longer coveted. Today, the beasts are prevalent in ponds and marshes throughout the Hudson Valley. Keep an eye out for their lodges, which resemble geodesic domes.

"In case the said island is inhabited by some Indians, these should not be driven away by force or threats, but should be persuaded by kind words or otherwise by giving them something to let us live amongst them." – Orders to Peter Minuit, New Netherland's director general, concerning Manhattan Island (1626)

Detail of WPA mural, Rhinebeck Post Office. Right: Manhattan Island.

Sole contemporary account of the island's purchase, written by Peter Schaghen to his bosses in the Dutch West India Company (1626)

High and Mighty Lords,

Yesterday the ship the Arms of Amsterdam arrived here. It sailed from New Netherland out of the River Mauritius on the 23d of September. They report that our people are in good spirit and live in peace. The women also have borne some children there. They have purchased the island Manhattes from the Indians for the value of 60 guilders. It is 11,000 morgens in size. They had all their grain sowed by the middle of May, and reaped by the middle of August. They sent samples of these summer grains: wheat, rye, barley, oats, buckwheat, canary seed, beans and flax.

The cargo of the aforesaid ship is: 7,246 beaver skins, 178 half otter skins, 675 otter skins, 48 mink skins, 36 lynx skins, 33 minks, 34 muskrat skins. Many oak timbers and nut wood.

Herewith, High and Mighty Lords, be commended to the mercy of the Almighty.

Your High and Mightinesses' obedient, P. Schaghen

In a deal that would make Donald Trump green with envy, Peter Minuit, New Netherland's director general, purchased Manhattan Island for the cost of an entrée in one of today's Midtown eateries. Of course, to the tribe that sold it – either the Shinnecock or Canarsie – the fabled $24 in goods and trinkets they received probably seemed like a bargain. After all, Native Americans had no notion of land ownership, and 22,000-acre Manhattan was so rocky and swarming with mosquitoes that you'd have to be nuts to want it.

The key to understanding the transaction, which took place shortly after Minuit's arrival in the colony on May 4, 1626, was that Netherlands' governing States General had ordered him to *buy* the land instead of taking it by force or squatting on it. It was an effort to live in peace with neighboring Native Americans.

The Manhattan acquisition set a precedent for future land deals: give a little, get a lot. How much? In a typical sale, Indians in 1677 received 40 kettles, 40 axes, four adzes, 40 shirts, 400 strings of white beads (for wampum), 800 strings of black beads, 50 pair of stockings, 100 bars of lead, one keg of powder, 100 knives, four quarter casks of wine, 40 jars, 60 cleaving knives, 60 blankets, 100 needles, 100 awls, and "one clean pipe" in return for *36,000 acres* between the Shawangunk Mountains and the Hudson River. While unfair, these purchases had the desired effect. Colonists of the Hudson Valley had fewer conflicts with Native Americans than French or English residents in nearby provinces.

On Manhattan, the city founded there – called New Amsterdam – wasted no time in becoming America's melting pot. This was largely the result of New Netherland's policy of religious tolerance and its reputation for being a meritocracy, a place where people who arrived with little but worked hard stood a good chance of climbing the colony's economic and social ladder. A visitor in 1646 was amazed to hear 18 languages spoken among the settlement's 500 inhabitants.

"Patroons of New Netherland shall be acknowledged those who will, within six years from this time, undertake to plant in New Netherland a Colony of forty-eight souls."

Peopling the colony: Agreement establishing the patroon system (1629)

FREEDOMS, PRIVILEGES and EXEMPTIONS granted by the High and Mighty Lords States General, *ex plenitudine potestatis,* to all persons of condition, inhabitants of these countries, to be qualified thereunto by their High Mightinesses, as Lords and Patroons of New Netherland, for the purpose of planting Colonies and introducing cattle there, all for the advancement of the Incorporated West India Company, and for the benefit of the inhabitants of these countries...

4. Lords and Patroons of New Netherland shall be acknowledged those who will, within six years from this time...undertake to plant in New Netherland a Colony of forty-eight souls, on pain, in case of palpable neglect, of being deprived, at their High Mightinesses' discretion, of their acquired Freedoms, Privileges and Exemptions...

6. And from the very moment that the Lords and Patroons of New Netherland have designated the places where they wish to plant their Colonies, and have obtained admission thereto from their High Mightinesses, they shall be preferred before all others, for such lands as they have selected.

7. But if they are not afterwards pleased with the places, or be deceived in the selection of the land, they shall have another opportunity to make a selection.

8. And the Patroons of New Netherland may, by Deputy, at the places where they will plant their Colonies, extend their limits six miles along the sea coast or on both sides of a navigable river, and so deep landward in, as the Lords and Patroons shall demand...

10. And in propriety forever and always possess, all the land situate within the Patroons' limits, together with all the fruits, superficies, minerals, rivers and fountains thereof, for them, their heirs or assigns...

13. The Patroons shall provisionally furnish proper instructions to their Colonies, in order that they be ruled and appointed, both in police and justice, conformably to the mode of government observed here...

22. No person shall be at liberty to take from the service of the Patroons any of their Colonists, whether man, woman, son, daughter, maid-servant, or man-servant, even though solicited by the Colonists themselves to receive them (except by written consent of their Patroons), during the term of years for which they are bound to their Patroons; after the expiration of which time, the Patroons shall be at liberty to send back to this country the Colonists who leave their service...

25. And if any Colonist belonging to a Patroon happen to discover minerals, precious stones, crystals, marble, pearl fishery or such like, they shall remain the Patroon's property, provided he allow such discoverer, as a premium therefore, so much as the Patroon shall have stipulated for that purpose...

27. The Patroons of New Netherland, shall be bound to purchase from the Lords Sachems in New Netherland, the soil where they propose to plant their Colonies, and shall acquire such right thereunto as they will agree for with the said Sachems...

30. Their High Mightinesses shall exert themselves to provide the Patroons with persons bound to service, who shall be obliged to serve out their bounden time, in all obedience, for their board and clothing only, which being done, on bringing to this country a certificate thereof from the Patroons or their Commissaries, such persons shall be here restored to their former state and freedom.

31. In like manner, the Incorporated West India Company shall allot to each Patroon twelve Black men and women out of the prizes in which Negroes shall be found, for the advancement of the Colonies in New Netherland...

Thus done and enacted.

Philipse Manor Hall, Yonkers. Left: RamsHorn-Livingston Sanctuary, once part of 160,000-acre Livingston Manor.

Unlike other American colonies, New Netherland was founded as a commercial venture, but the Dutch West India Company soon realized that it needed people to exploit its investment. The land was primed for habitation. All of the basic food groups were plentiful – there were fruits, nuts, grains, and game galore. There also was acre upon acre of choice land just waiting to be cleared and cultivated. All that was needed was a way to get fledgling farmers onto the boats – while holding down the company's expenses.

Jeweler Killiaen Van Rensselaer, a company founder, came up with a solution: the patroon system. Established in 1629, it granted near-feudal rights to any wealthy merchant – or patroon – who agreed to populate the valley. In exchange for taking on the costs of establishing mini-colonies of 48 or more settlers, the patroons were allowed to negotiate with the Indians for the purchase of huge tracts of land, which by law would remain in their families forever. The Dutch formally granted five valley patroonships, the succeeding English (who called them manors) four more.

Tenant farmers living under the yoke of these aristocratic landlords were forced to pay yearly rents, render up to a tenth of all produce grown, and do several days work annually on the estate – clearing roads, cutting and hauling firewood, etc. From farmsteads they'd laboriously hacked out of the wilderness, they occasionally carped about the status quo. The patroons displayed little sympathy. "Our people are hoggish and brutish," wrote Philip Livingston, second Lord of Livingston Manor, in 1740. "They must be humbl'd." The patroon system survived the American Revolution and continued until the 1840s, when it came to a cataclysmic end.

Perhaps not so surprising, Van Rensselaer was awarded the valley's first patroonship in 1630, although he never left the Netherlands. Instead, he instructed his agent, Bastiaen Krol, to purchase his fiefdom from the Iroquois Nation. Krol wound up amassing more than 700,000 acres in present-day Albany, Rensselaer, and Columbia counties, making Van Rensselaer the New World's first real estate tycoon.

"The Esopus savages shall not come armed to the Dutch plantations, houses and habitations, but without arms they may go, come and trade as before."

Peter Stuyvesant's treaty with the Esopus Indians (1660)

Articles of peace, made at the request of the below named chiefs of the savages between the Hon. *Petrus Stuyvesant*, Director-General of *New-Netherland* and the Sachems or chiefs of the Indians of the *Esopus*.

1. All hostilities on either side shall cease and all acts and injuries shall be forgotten and forgiven by either side.

2. The *Esopus* savages promise to convey, as indemnification, to the aforesaid Director-General all the territory of the *Esopus* and to remove to a distance from there, without ever returning again to plant.

3. They promise further to pay to the said Director-General in return for the ransom, taken for the captured Christians, 500 schepels of Indian corn, one half during the next fall, when the corn is ripe, the other half or its value during the fall next following.

4. The *Esopus* savages promise to keep this treaty inviolable, not to kill horses, cattle, hogs nor even a chicken or if it should happen to be done, then the chiefs undertake to pay for it and in case of refusal one of them shall be kept in prison or under arrest until the loss has been paid or made good, which on the other side the Director-General promises, that the *Dutch* neither shall be permitted to do any harm to them.

5. If the *Dutch* should kill a savage or the savages a Dutchman, war shall not be immediately commenced again for that reason, but a complaint shall be made and the murderers shall be delivered to be punished, as they deserve.

6. The *Esopus* savages shall not come armed to the *Dutch* plantations, houses and habitations, but without arms they may go, come and trade as before.

7. Whereas the last war was caused by drunken people, no savage shall be allowed to drink brandy or strong liquor in or near the *Dutch* plantations, houses or settlements, but he must go with it to his land or to some distant place in the woods.

8. Included in this peace shall be all, not only the aforementioned tribes of savages, but also all others, who are in friendship with the Director-General, among others especially the chief of *Long-Island, Tapousagh* and all his savages; if any act of hostility should be committed against these, the Director-General would consider it his duty, to assist them.

9. The aforesaid chiefs, as mediators and advocates of the *Esopus* tribe, remain bondsmen and engage themselves, to have this treaty kept inviolate and in the case the *Esopus* Indians should break the peace now concluded, they undertake altogether to assist the *Dutch* to subdue the *Esopus* savages.

10. On the foregoing conditions the said Director-General offered first to the aforesaid mediators and they accepted each a piece of cloth and to the chiefs of the *Esopus* savages 3 of their captives and each a piece of cloth.

Thus done and concluded at the settlement on the *Esopus*, under the blue sky, in the presence of the Hon. *Marten Cregier*, Burgomaster of the City of *Amsterdam* in *New-Netherland*, *Oloff Stevenson Cortland*, ex-Burgomaster, *Arent van Curler*, deputy of the Colony of *Renselaerswyck* and many people of the *Esopus*, both Christians and Indians, the 15th July 1660.

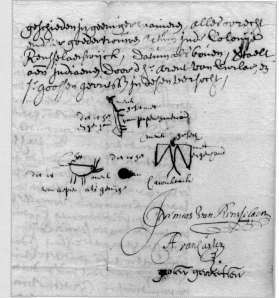

Native American and Dutch signatures on 1663 land deed (courtesy Albany Institute of History & Art Library). Right: Native American Festival at Saratoga Spa State Park.

As New Netherland expanded into the frontier – and onto the Native Americans' hunting grounds – conflicts became more frequent. Around Wiltwyck (today's Kingston), the Esopus Indians waged vicious warfare for two years, burning farmhouses and taking prisoners until peg-legged Peter Stuyvesant, the colony's director general, negotiated a treaty in 1660.

As part of the settlement, all Dutch captives but one were returned. The lone holdout, states an early account, had taken an Indian wife "who became pregnant, and [was] unwilling to part with him or he with her." Eleven Native Americans captured by the Dutch also were not returned. They had been shipped as slaves to Curaçao. The peace lasted just three years. In 1663, the Indians torched the stockaded Dutch settlement before agreeing to a more lasting treaty.

The Esopus were a tribe of the Algonguian-speaking people, whose villages once lined the shores of this waterway they called *Muhheakunnuk* – the river that flows both ways. (From its mouth up to the city of Troy, the Hudson is actually a tidal estuary, an inland arm of the Atlantic Ocean.) Diseases introduced by the Dutch, the vast size of colonial land purchases, and warfare with neighboring Mohawks either wiped them out or forced them to migrate. By 1700, 90 percent of the valley's Native American population – once perhaps as high as 20,000 – had disappeared.

All that's left of these first inhabitants are pictographs on fading documents – the signatures of chiefs who dealt with the Dutch – and the colorful place names they bestowed. From Ossining (stone upon stone) and Kerhonkson (wild geese) to Cohoes (canoe falling) and Coxsackie (owl's hoot), these names keep us in touch with the distant past.

"It's easy to cut big chunks from someone else's cheese."

The police blotter: Cases from Fort Orange court records (1656-1657)

Complaint against Hendrick Hendrickson, baker, for selling bread below the regular weight; fined and suspended from following his business.

Sentence. Dirckje Harmens for selling beer to Indians; fined 300 guilders.

Suit against Jellis Fonda's wife for removing Lewis Cobussen's wife's petticoat from the fence; defendant says plaintiff pawned the article for beaver; put over.

Goosen Gerritsen against Jurriaen Jansen, for having circulated a report that he was betrothed to Annetie Lievens, the plaintiff's bride; defendant acknowledges circulating the report and its falsehood, but pleads that he had been instigated thereto by Cornelis Teunissen; ordered to prove this allegation.

The sheriff against Hendrick Andriessen, for standing in the middle of the street at ten o'clock at night with a drawn cutlass in his hand.

Action of slander. Ulderick Kleyn against Eldert Gerbertsen, for stating that his wife had been whipped and branded on the scaffold at Amsterdam; defendant pleads provocation, having been abused by the woman.

Abraham Pietersen Vosbergh against Cobus Teunissen and Tjerck Claessen for carrying off a tree he had cut down for building purposes; judgment for defendants on the ground that the tree had been cut down three years.

Complaint against Jan the weaver for selling liquor after the ringing of the bell and during sermon; fined.

Maretje Claessen against Wynant Gerritsen, defamation, for calling her a thief, and accusing her of having stolen defendant's hen; defendant makes reparation and is fined 12 guilders for the poor.

Complaint against Adriaen Jansen from Leyden for sending an Indian broker into the woods to trade with Indians, and for taking beavers from a squaw by force and thrusting her out of doors; case put over.

Anyone who's gazed upon 17th-century genre paintings from the Netherlands knows that the Dutch were a fun-loving, gregarious people. Obviously, life in the New World was no different from that in the Old. Visitors to New Netherland often commented on the settlers' penchant for spirited talk. Perched on benches built into the stoops of their homes – America's first front porches – town residents carried on nightly gabfests. "In the evening these seats are covered with people of both sexes; but this is rather troublesome, as those who pass are obliged to greet every body, unless they will shock the politeness of the inhabitants of this town," wrote Swedish botanist Peter Kalm during a visit to Albany in 1749, when Dutch customs still prevailed.

What did they talk about? Just what we do – local gossip. If Fort Orange court records are any indication, the colonial sheriff and judge were the busiest people in town. Accounts of their activities still make entertaining reading. They also point up the interesting fact that the women of New Netherland enjoyed a level of independence unheard of in other American colonies. For example, it not only was legally possible but socially acceptable for them to conduct their own business transactions. (The most successful female merchant was Margaret Hardenbroeck Philipse, who managed a fleet of trading vessels.) With the colony's English takeover, many of these liberties quickly disappeared.

Another prime topic of conversation among the Dutch was food. Old sayings handed down are peppered with references to comestibles consumed in their daily diet.

Inside their steeply gabled townhouses – some of the earliest were built of bricks used as ballast in ships – the few rooms were sparsely furnished but spotless, a testament to the Dutch housewife's industriousness. "The women…rise early, go to sleep very late, and are almost over nice and cleanly in regard to the floor, which is frequently scoured several times in the week," enthused Kalm. Most activity was centered in the spacious "great room," which served as kitchen-living room-bedroom-rumpus room. Step through the two-part Dutch door on the home of a prosperous burgher, and you might see the main fireplace surrounded with Delft tiles depicting biblical or other scenes, a sign of wealth and a nostalgic nod to the mother country.

Dutch food-based sayings

"Even if it rained milk, his bowls would be upside down."
His luck is always bad.

"He talks like a sausage without the fat."
He's a man of few words.

"It's easy to cut big chunks from someone else's cheese."
It's more fun to spend money if it's not your own.

"When butter gets expensive, you learn to eat your bread dry."
Economize during hard times.

"The way you choose a melon, you should choose your friends."
Select your friends carefully.

Old Dutch Church, Sleepy Hollow. Left: Weaver at Philipsburg Manor.

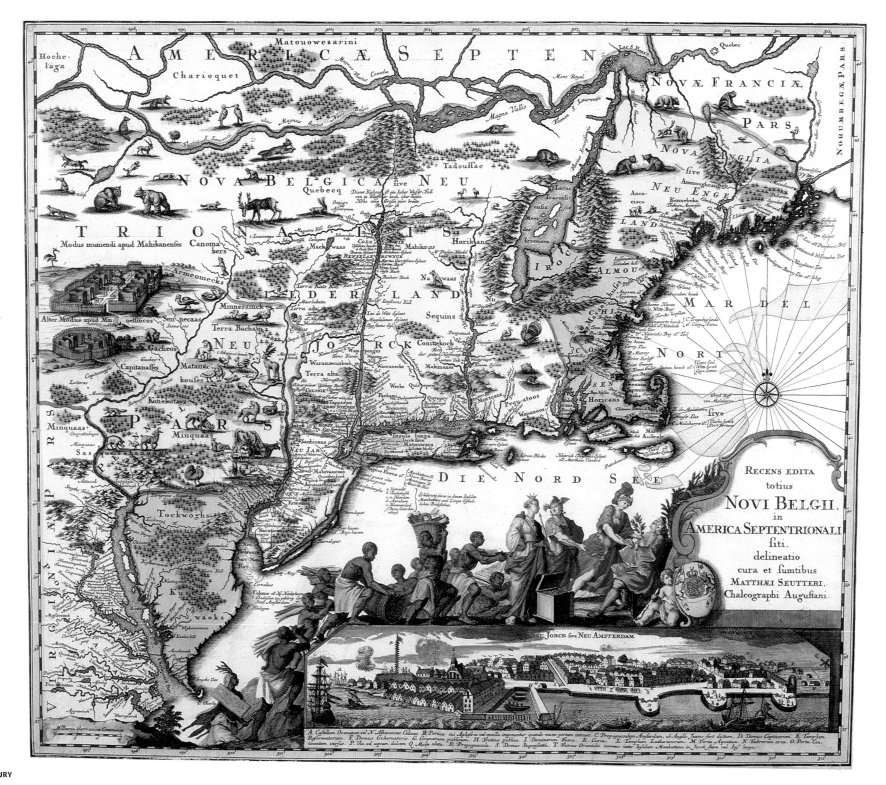

"All people shall still continue free denizens and enjoy their lands, houses, goods, ships, wheresoever they are within this country."

Circa-1630 Van Rensselaer cannon, New York State Museum. Left: Colonial map, courtesy Historic Hudson Valley.

Articles of Capitulation on the Reduction of New Netherland (1664)

1. We consent that the States-General or West India Company shall freely enjoy all farms and houses (except such as are in the forts), and that within six months they shall have free liberty to transport all such arms and ammunition as now do belong to them, or else they shall be paid for them.

2. All public houses shall continue for the uses which they are now for.

3. All people shall still continue free denizens and enjoy their lands, houses, goods, ships, wheresoever they are within this country, and dispose of them as they please.

4. If any inhabitant have a mind to remove himself he shall have a year and six weeks from this day to remove himself, wife, children, servants, goods, and to dispose of his lands here…

6. It is consented to, that any people may freely come from the Netherlands and plant in this country, and that Dutch vessels may freely come hither, and any of the Dutch may freely return home, or send any sort of merchandise home in vessels of their own country.

7. All ships from the Netherlands, or any other place, and goods therein, shall be received here and sent hence after the manner which formerly they were before our coming hither for six months next ensuing.

8. The Dutch here shall enjoy the liberty of their consciences in Divine Worship and church discipline.

9. No Dutchman here, or Dutch ship here, shall, upon any occasion, be prest to serve in war, against any nation whatever.

10. That the townsmen of the Manhatoes shall not have any soldier quartered upon them without being satisfied and paid for them by their officers…

11. The Dutch here shall enjoy their own customs concerning their inheritances…

13. No judgment that hath passed any judicature here shall be called in question, but if any conceive that he hath not had justice done him, if he apply himself to the States-General the other party shall be bound to answer for ye supposed injury.

14. If any Dutch living here shall, at any time, desire to travel or traffic into England, or any place or plantation in obedience to his Majesty of England, or with the Indians, he shall have (upon his request to the Governor) a certificate that he is a free denizen of this place, and liberty to do so…

16. All inferior civil officers and magistrates shall continue as now they are (if they please), till the customary time of new election, and then new ones to be chosen, by themselves, provided that such new chosen magistrates shall take the oath of allegiance to his Majesty of England before they enter upon their office…

19. The officers, military and soldiers, shall march out, with their arms, drums beating and colors flying, and lighted matches, and if any of them will plant they shall have 50 acres of land set out for them, if any of them will serve any as servants, they shall continue with all safety, and become free denizens afterwards.

20. If at any time hereafter the King of Great Britain and the States of the Netherland, do agree that this place and country be re-delivered into the hands of the said States whensoever his Majesty will send his commands to re-deliver it, it shall immediately be done.

21. That the town of Manhatans shall choose Deputies, and those Deputies shall have free voices in all public affairs, as much as any other Deputies…

On these articles being consented to and signed by Col. Richard Nicolls, Deputy Governor to his Royal Highness, within two hours after, the fort and town called New Amsterdam, upon the Isle of Manhatoes, shall be delivered into the hands of the said Col Richard Nicolls by the service of such as shall be by him.

Did success spoil New Netherland? In the 1660s, trade was booming at the port of New Amsterdam. In addition to making money off the Hudson Valley's produce and natural resources, the city was siphoning off a tenth of all profits from the lucrative tobacco markets in nearby British colonies. England was not amused. It was time for a takeover.

Great Britain's desire to build a North American empire called for westward expansion through the Hudson Valley. The only obstacle was the Dutch fort at New Amsterdam. It turned out to be a paper tiger, undermanned and in deplorable condition.

In the end, Dutch rule vanished without so much as a whimper. All it took was the arrival of four British warships and two suggestions from Richard Nicolls, who commanded the fleet: 1) if the Dutch didn't capitulate, his soldiers would loot the city; and 2) England was willing to let the Dutch continue trading with their homeland. That was enough for the city's pragmatic merchants. Ninety-three of them signed a petition calling on Peter Stuyvesant to surrender. It's said that the feisty director general tore up the articles of capitulation, exclaiming he'd "much rather be carried out dead." The determined burghers pieced the document back together and convinced him to sign.

The colony was ceded to Great Britain on September 8, 1664. It was immediately rechristened New York, after James Stuart, the Duke of York and Albany, whose brother, King George II, had granted him a royal charter. The extremely generous surrender agreement, said to be a precursor to the American Bill of Rights, went a long way toward fostering respect and cooperation between the Dutch and English.

"The easiest way to feel in contact with the 17th century is by scanning the phone book."

While traces of New Netherland may not be as prevalent as they were during Franklin Roosevelt's boyhood – he recalled hearing Dutch still being spoken – they survive all around us. Travel down any rural road and you're likely to see a house built by one of the early settlers from stones gathered in nearby fields. These sturdy, squat dwellings look for all the world like glacial erratics, those huge boulders left behind as the last Ice Age retreated.

Centuries-old cemeteries – such as those in Sleepy Hollow, Fishkill, and Kingston – also bear witness to our 17th-century past. Their headstones, the text inscribed in Dutch, are often carved with ghoulish death's heads or smiling angels. At the Albany Institute of History & Art, you can gaze into the eyes of early colonists as portrayed by some of North America's first painters. While these works hardly compare artistically to the masterpieces of Rembrandt, their primitive quality captures the fortitude these settlers needed to tame such a wilderness. Also in Albany, the Tulip Festival – celebrated each May, when Washington Park is ablaze with thousands of the flowers so prized by the Dutch – provides a colorful way of remembering the city's history.

But the easiest way to feel in contact with the 17th century is by scanning the phone books of Dutch-named towns like Yonkers, Saugerties, and Kinderhook. They contain names brought to these shores on the first ships – Van Dusen, Van Kleeck, Van Rensselaer, Van Keuren… Which just goes to show this is no ho-hum history. In fact, it's just a phone call away.

Dutch was still the language of choice for the Brinckerhoff family in 1754; from the Fishkill First Reformed Church graveyard. Right: Captain William Reynolds of the New Netherland Museum's replica ship *Half Moon* presents cruise certificates earned by Albany-area students during a weeklong voyage of discovery on the Hudson.

Winter

Preceding pages: Hoarfrost and snow coat Bear Mountain.

Seasonal sports – Taking to the slopes at Hunter Mountain in the Catskills; an historic ice yacht glides at 60 m.p.h. across Tivoli Bay.

From Albany's Empire State Plaza, flanking the state capitol (above), to Manhattan's Rockefeller Center, skaters enjoy the valley's deep freeze.

Keeping commerce flowing – A Coast Guard ice-breaking buoy tender clears a channel for a tugboat heading past the historic Hudson-Athens Lighthouse; an Amtrak train carrying passengers from Albany, Chicago, and points west speeds through the snow-covered Hudson Highlands.

Ulster County's Rondout Creek (above) flows directly into the Hudson at Kingston; the yield of Westchester County's environmentally protected Croton River watershed, captured by the Croton Dam, flows into New York City's faucets.

At Mills Mansion, a state historic site in Staatsburg, the dining room evokes the Gilded Age; the lawn invites youthful exuberance.

The 18th Century

"I think, considering the great toils we have undergone, the roughness of some parts of this country, and our original poverty, that we have done the most in the least time of any people on earth."

From *Letters From an American Farmer* by Orange County resident J. Hector St. Jean de Crevecoeur (1769)

The great objects which an American farmer ought to have in view are simplicity of labour and dispatch. The sun, and the great vegetation which it causes, hurry him along. The multiplicity of business which crowds all at the same time is astonishing. This is the principal reason why we can do nothing so neatly as you do in Europe. Could we fallow cut wheat-land in the fall, this would greatly relieve us in the summer. We are, therefore, often obliged to keep double-teams in order to accelerate our operations. What I mean by simplicity is the art of doing a great deal with few hands. For that reason, I am extremely fond of ploughing with three horses abreast because it is a powerful team and requires but one person. I have heard many Europeans blame us for many of our operations. Alas, they censured us before they knew anything of our climate, of our seasons, and the scarcity and dearness of labourers. I think, considering our age, the great toils we have undergone, the roughness of some parts of this country, and our original poverty, that we have done the most in the least time of any people on earth. Call it industry or what you will.

The barn, with regard to its situation, size, convenience, and good finishing is an object, in the mind of a farmer, superior even to that of his dwelling. Many don't care much how they are lodged, provided that they have a good barn and barn-yard, and indeed it is the criterion by which I always judge a farmer's prosperity. On this building he never begrudges his money. The middle-sized ones are commonly fifty by thirty feet; mine is sixty by thirty-five and cost two hundred and twenty dollars. They are either shingled, clapboarded, or boarded on the outside. Therein we lodge all our grain; and within, many operations are performed, such as threshing, and cleaning of flax and husking the corn, etc. Therein the horses are stabled and the oxen stall-fed. In the summer, the women resort to it in order to spin their wool. The neatness of our boarded floors, the great draught of air caused by the opened doors, which are always made wide enough to permit a loaded wagon to enter, and their breadth afford [the women] an opportunity of spinning long threads, or carding at their ease. Many farmers have several barracks in their barn-yards where they put their superfluous hay and straw. Nor ought the subdivision of these yards to pass unnoticed. They require great judgment, demand attention and expense. All classes of our cattle, our sheep, our calves must be placed by themselves, and have in each division convenient racks and bars in order to communicate easily from one to another.

By the mid-18th century, the Hudson Valley was the breadbasket of the American colonies. "The wheat flour from Albany is reckoned the best in North America, except that from Sopus [Esopus] or King's Town [Kingston]," wrote Swedish visitor Peter Kalm in 1749. Valley soils were perfect for sowing the crop – farmers reaped up to 20 bushels of grain for each bushel of seed planted. Abundant, fast-running steams provided power for gristmills.

Farm families didn't lack for delicious, nutritious food. In their kitchen gardens, the first in the New World, the transplanted Dutch cultivated cabbages and carrots, artichokes and onions, parsnips and parsley. Potatoes, introduced on valley farms in the 18th century, quickly became a staple. Every farm had livestock; the colony's first shipment of horses and cattle – 103 head – arrived in 1625. Also on board was a sizeable herd of sheep and pigs. By 1708, local farmers reaped enough wool and flax each year to produce three-quarters of the colony's cloth.

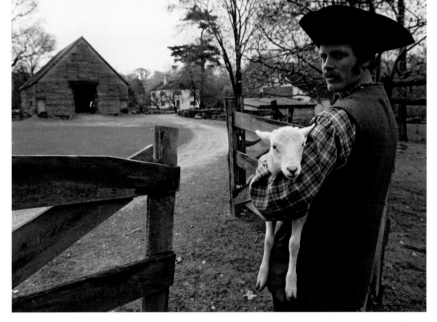

Farm at Philipsburg Manor. Left: Marlboro orchards.

Farmers relied on their barns. Well into the 19th century, many were built in the square Dutch style, with a wide central aisle and narrow side bays. The importance of these structures can be seen in their architectural framing, which bears a striking resemblance to Gothic cathedrals. Like the medieval churches, they were built to last. Quite a few still grace valley farmsteads today.

Agriculture continued flourishing in the Hudson Valley until the second half of the 20th century. But by 1997, fields were becoming subdivisions so rapidly that the American Farmland Trust ranked the region's farms among the nation's most endangered. A concerted effort to protect them was begun. Today, 1,000 square miles of farmland remain, but the crops are more varied – from goats whose milk yields award-winning cheeses and wineries producing vintages that compare favorably with California's best, to potential Kentucky Derby winners and micro-greens fought over by Manhattan's top chefs.

"From the very beginning, the valley's riches have brought out the best ideas in people."

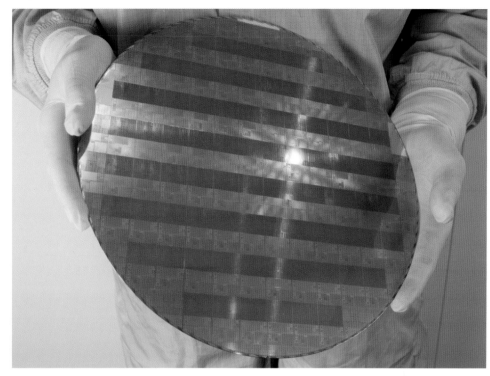

Chinese export porcelain depicts East-West trade (courtesy Historic Hudson Valley); a 300-mm wafer yields scores of IBM supercomputer processing chips. Left: "Dressing" a millstone at Philipsburg Manor.

It's been said that a nation's wealth depends on how creatively it uses its natural resources. No wonder the Hudson Valley has been such an economic engine. From the very beginning, its riches have brought out the best ideas in people.

Take the Hudson River, America's first sea-level waterway, stretching 150 miles inland from New York Harbor. In the 18th century, the Hudson River sloop was specially crafted to handle the tides and tricky winds. It quickly became the workhorse of commerce, turning once-sleepy waterfront villages into thriving ports. In the 20th century, a deep-water channel was dredged so eight-story freighters can follow Henry Hudson's route and dock near Albany's original trading post. In 2005 alone, more than 579,000 tons of cargo – everything from molasses and aluminum to cocoa beans and salt – passed through the Port of Albany, on its way to or from Nigeria, Indonesia, Sweden, and dozens of other countries.

Even the valley's rocks yield bonanzas. Beginning in the 18th century, the hard conglomerate bedrock of the Shawangunks was fashioned into millstones. They were used to process a chief contribution to America's triangular trade, whereby profits from the sale of flour shipped to Europe bought manufactured goods exchanged in Africa for slaves to toil in local fields. Later in the century, iron ore from its hills was used to produce the great chain intended to block British ships at West Point during the American Revolution. Weighing 65 tons, the chain was forged at the valley's Sterling Furnace in 1778. It was completed in less than three months – ahead of schedule and under budget – making it one of America's first great manufacturing triumphs. Today, silica, the basic element of all rocks, is used by IBM technicians in East Fishkill to create high-density chips capable of processing millions of messages from across the globe in nanoseconds.

Henry Hudson never discovered a Northwest Passage, but he did find a remarkable valley. Today, IBM experts in Hudson's valley are crafting the quickest route to China – and everywhere else.

"The Freeholders and inhabitants of Coxsackie associate under the Ties of Religion, Honor and Love of our Country to adopt and endeavor to carry into Execution whatever Measures may be rendered by our Continental Congress."

Supporting the Continental Congress: The Coxsackie Declaration of Independence (1775)

Persuaded that the Salvation of the Rights and Liberties of America, depends, under God, on the firm union of its inhabitants, in a vigorous prosecution of the Measures necessary for its Safety, and convinced of the Necessity of preventing the Anarchy and confusion which attend the Dissolution of the Powers of Government:

That the Freeholders and inhabitants of Coxsackie District, in the County of Albany, being greatly alarmed at the avowed Design of the Ministry to raise a Revenue in America, are shocked by the bloody Scene acting in the Massachusetts Bay; Do in the most solemn manner, resolve never to become Slaves; and do also associate under the Ties of Religion, Honor and Love of our Country to adopt and endeavor to carry into Execution whatever Measures may be rendered by our Continental Congress, or resolved upon by our Provincial convention for the purpose of preserving our Constitution and opposing the Execution of several arbitrary and oppressive Acts of the British Parliament, until a reconciliation between Great Britain and America or constitution principles (which we most ardently desire) can be obtained; and that we will, in all Things, follow the advice of our general Committee, respecting the purpose aforesaid, the preservation of Peace and good Order, and the Safety of Individuals and private property.

Dated at Coxsackie the Seventeenth of May in the Year of our Lord, One Thousand seven hundred and seventy five.

The king's citizens respond: The Loyalist Declaration of Dependence, signed in British-held Manhattan (1776)

November 28, 1776

May it please your Excellencies.

Impressed with the most grateful sense of the Royal Clemency, manifested in your Proclamation of the 14th of July last, whereby His Majesty hath been graciously pleased to declare, "That he is desirous to deliver His American subjects from the calamities of War, and other oppressions, which they now undergo:" and equally affected with sentiments of gratitude for that generous and humane attention to the happiness of these Colonies, which distinguishes your Excellencies subsequent Declaration, evincing your disposition "to confer with His Majesty's well affected subjects, upon the means of restoring the public Tranquility, and establishing a permanent union with every Colony as a part of the British Empire."

We whose names are hereunto subscribed, Inhabitants of the city and County of New York, beg leave to inform your Excellencies: that although most of us have subscribed a general Representation with many others of the Inhabitants; yet we wish that our conduct, in maintaining inviolate our loyalty to our Sovereign, against the strong tide of oppression and tyranny, which had almost overwhelmed this Land, may be marked by some line of distinction, which cannot well be drawn from the mode of Representation that has been adopted for the Inhabitants in general.

Influenced by this Principle, and from a regard to our peculiar Situation, we have humbly presumed to trouble your Excellencies with the second application; in which, we flatter ourselves, none participate but those who have ever, with unshaken fidelity, borne true Allegiance to His Majesty, and the most warm and affectionate attachment to his Person and Government. That, notwithstanding the tumult of the times, and the extreme difficulties and losses to which many of us have been exposed, we have always expressed, and do now give this Testimony of our Zeal to preserve and support the Constitutional Supremacy of Great Britain over the Colonies; and do most ardently wish for a speedy restoration of that union between them, which, while it subsisted, proved the unfailing source of their mutual happiness and prosperity...

While the Revolution's first shots were fired in Massachusetts, it could be said that the war began in New York. Rumblings of rebellion were felt as early as 1765, when the city turned out in force to protest the Stamp Tax – London's first imposition of "taxation without representation" on its American colonies. (The money was needed to pay for the French and Indian War.) A mob attacked the royal arsenal, where the stamps were stored, and torched the home of its commander, who had threatened to stuff the stamps down residents' throats with his sword. The tax was revoked the following year.

Fast forward to July 9, 1776, when a throng listening to a reading of the Declaration of Independence surged down Broadway and toppled a statue of King George. The lead sculpture was melted down and recast as musket balls for American troops, who'd soon need them. That summer, a fleet of 250 British warships and transports – the largest armada in English history – arrived in New York Harbor. On board were 32,000 crack soldiers itching to put a quick end to the rebellion. By winter, they'd driven George Washington's Continentals from New York City. It would remain in British hands until 1783, when General Washington led his triumphant troops back into Manhattan.

The American Revolution was our first civil war: Some family members sided with the Continental Congress, while others remained loyal to King George III. As in Iraq, much of the violence took place far from battlefields. Patriot residents of Westchester County, the "neutral ground" abutting British-held Manhattan, fell prey to foraging parties of loyalists dubbed "cowboys." On valley frontiers, homesteads faced threats of sneak attacks from pro-English Iroquois.

Both sides took up the pen. A year before the Declaration of Independence was drafted in Philadelphia, 225 farmers in Coxsackie expressed their displeasure with the British Parliament. Unable to write their names, some signed the document with a "+." A year later, more than 500 New York City residents – including Frederick Philipse III, lord of Philipsburg Manor – registered their allegiance to the crown by affixing their John Hancocks to a Declaration of *Dependence*. By war's end, they'd be among 35,000 loyalist New Yorkers forced to flee their homeland forever.

Reenactment of 1777 Battle of Kingston by the British Brigade.
Inset: Uniform buttons of the Revolution: RP – Royal Provincials, worn by loyalist soldiers; USA, worn by the Continental Army.

"Treason of the blackest dye was yesterday discovered."

An American hero: Benedict Arnold leads the charge at the Second Battle of Saratoga. From Benson Lossing's *Pictorial Field-Book of the Revolution* (1859)

General Arnold had watched with eager eye and excited spirit the course of the battle thus far. Deprived of all command, he had not authority even to *fight*, much less to *order*. Smarting under the indignity heaped upon him by his commander…and stirred by the din of battle around him, the brave soldier became fairly maddened by his emotions and, leaping upon his large brown horse, he started off on a full gallop for the field of conflict. Gates immediately sent Major Armstrong after him to order him back. Arnold saw him approaching…spurred his horse and left his pursuer far behind, while he placed himself at the head of three regiments of Learned's brigade, who received their former commander with loud huzzas. He immediately led them against the British center, and, with the desperation of a madman, rushed into the thickest of the fight…

The conflict was now terrible indeed, and in the midst of the…smoke and metal hail, Arnold was conspicuous. His voice, clear as a trumpet, animated the soldiers, and, as if ubiquitous, he seemed to be every where amid the perils at the same moment. With a part of the brigades of Patterson and Glover, he assaulted the works occupied by the light infantry under Earl Balcarras, and at the point of the bayonet drove the enemy from a strong abates, through which he attempted to force his way into the camp. He was obliged to abandon the effort, and, dashing forward toward the right flank of the enemy, exposed to the cross-fire of the contending armies, he met Learned's brigade advancing to make an assault upon the British works at an opening in the abates, between Balcarras's light infantry and the German right flank defence under Colonel Breyman[n]…

Arnold placed himself at the head of the brigade and moved rapidly on to the attack…. Having found the sally-port, he rushed within the enemy's intrenchments. The Germans, who had seen him upon his steed in the thickest of the fight for more than two hours, terrified at his approach, fled in dismay, delivering a volley in their retreat, which killed Arnold's horse under him, and wounded the general himself very severely…in the leg. Here, wounded and disabled…Arnold was overtaken by Major Armstrong, who delivered to him Gates's order to return to camp, fearing he "might do some rash thing!" He indeed did a rash thing: He led troops to victory without an order from his commander.

Arnold the traitor: Selling Fortress West Point to the British. Major General Nathanael Greene's Order of the Day (September 26, 1780)

Treason of the blackest dye was yesterday discovered. General Arnold, who commanded at West Point, lost to every sentiment of honor, of public and private obligation, was about to deliver up that important fort into the hands of the enemy. Such an event must have given the American cause a deadly wound if not a fatal stab. Happily the scheme was timely discovered to prevent the final misfortune. The providential train of circumstances which led to it affords the most convincing proofs that the liberties of America are the object of divine protection. At the same time the treason is so regretted the General cannot help congratulating the army on the happy discovery.

Our enemies, despairing of carrying their point by force, are practicing every base art to effect, by bribery and corruption, what they cannot accomplish in a manly way. Great honor is due to the American army that this is the first instance of treason of this kind, where many were to be expected from the nature of the dispute, and nothing is so high an ornament to the characters of the American soldiers as their withstanding all the arts and seductions of an insidious enemy.

It's hard to come to grips with Benedict Arnold, the hero whose name became a synonym for "traitor."

One thing's for sure: Arnold loved being in the thick of things. At Saratoga, his exploits played a major role in halting a British invasion from Canada intent on dividing the 13 colonies by securing control of the Hudson River. Arnold distinguished himself in the first battle on September 19, 1777. When a second battle brewed on October 7, his jealous commander ordered him to stay in his tent. But Arnold impetuously (some say drunkenly) rode off and led the troops in an action that resulted in the eventual British surrender. He deserves kudos for achieving this "turning point of the American Revolution," which proved that the ragtag "rebels" could beat the world's best-trained army. Just as important, the victory guaranteed France's entry into the war as our ally.

Cannons at Saratoga Battlefield. Left: Fort Putnam, the main defensive fortification of Revolutionary War West Point.

Arnold always had a chip on his shoulder. By 1780, he was fuming because of slights that impeded his promotion. Wangling command of Fortress West Point – a ring of fortifications surrounding the great iron chain stretched across the Hudson – he agreed to surrender this "American Gibraltar" to the British for 20,000 pounds. The plot was foiled when Arnold's British intermediary, Major John André, was captured with the general's handwritten plans to the fortress hidden in his boot. André was hanged. Arnold escaped and became a British officer.

Despite his perfidy, Arnold's valor was too vital to victory to be completely expunged. So he has been honored in anonymity. A wordless monument bearing a likeness of Arnold's right leg, shattered by a musket ball while leading a charge, stands on the Saratoga Battlefield (now a national historic site). And in the old Cadet Chapel at the U.S. Military Academy on West Point, plaques honor all the Continental major generals. Arnold's bears only his rank and birth date, no name or date of death.

Even at the scene of his crime, the traitor gets a backhanded thanks.

"Our troops advanced with the greatest regularity and firmness without firing a gun or once breaking their order."

An eyewitness account of the battle of Stony Point by an anonymous Continental officer (1779)

Since my last I have been engaged in one of the most serious and fortunate transactions of my life; I mean attacking the works on Stony Point by storm.

On the 15th inst. At 12 o'clock, about 1,150 of chosen troops, the light infantry of our army, Commanded by Brig. General Wayne, marched from this place, arrived within two miles of Stony Point by sunset, and made disposition for attacking at midnight, viz.: a solid column of 700 men to go below the fort, march up the bank of the river, and attack it on the south side, 300 in columns to attack it the north side, about 150 to make a feint of attacking in front. From these columns was detached parties to cover the heads of them, cut away pickets, and remove impassable obstructions. At 12 o'clock we came across the enemy's picket guard, about half a mile from the fort, who fired on us and retired to the fort without our taking any notice of them.

Exactly at half-past 12 (I looked at my watch), the enemy fired generally on us from all their works as the front of the large column (in which I was) had got to the first line of abatTis, in about ten rods of the out works of the fort. The fire was very brisk from cannon and grape shot and lagrange, as well as from small arms with ball and buck shot, through which our troops advanced with the greatest regularity and firmness without firing a gun or once breaking their order, except to climb the abatTis, and then formed instantly after passing them, till a part of us forced into their works over the parapet and a part through their sally port. A little small arm firing and considerable bayoneting closed the scene exactly at 1 o'clock, where we remained under arms and the enemy under guard 'till daylight.

I was surprized when I viewed in the morning the difficulties our troops surmounted. The situation of ground was one of the strongest that nature ever form'd; three sides of it was surrounded by water, which was guarded by the shipping; the other side was a deep, miry, marsh, which was from water to water, making the point an island, which is rocky highlight of difficult access. Through the marsh we waded (which was up to my waist), directly under one of the enemy's works, which kept an incessant fire on us, and the abbatis lay on the bank of the marsh. This piece of ground was fortified by all British art and industry; two lines of their abatTis extended quite across the point into the river each way, and in the places easiest of approach was three lines besides the common breastworks…

I cannot help observing that so closely connected is humanity with real bravery, that notwithstanding the depredation the enemy had lately committed in our State, the cruelties our soldiers have suffered from them, and the works carried wholly by storm, yet I believe not one of the enemy was hurt after he had thrown down his arms and asked for quarter…

Americans needed a pick-me-up. Their Continental Army had been lackluster since Saratoga, and by 1779 they were eager for the war to end. Desperate for a rallying point – something to provide renewed faith in the cause – the eyes of Commander in Chief George Washington lit upon the British fortress at Stony Point, located just a dozen miles downriver from West Point.

The outpost seemed impregnable, akin to a medieval castle. It sat atop a rocky peninsula along the Hudson. A steep slope impeded access from the water, while swamps hampered attack on its flanks. The only easy means of entry was a heavily guarded causeway. Taking it would be a real coup.

Washington left nothing to chance. Infantrymen handpicked for the mission underwent two weeks of drilling under the demanding Friedrich von Steuben, the Prussian drillmaster who'd turned the undisciplined Continental Army into a cohesive fighting unit. And to lead the assault, he chose Brigadier General Anthony Wayne, whose nickname – "Mad Anthony" – was rumored to be a tribute to his penchant for allowing his men little sleep. At Stony Point, this quality came in handy: Washington planned the attack for midnight on July 16th.

It was unlike any other battle the Americans fought, resembling a Special Forces operation. It relied on stealth, speed, subterfuge – and utter silence. The soldiers were ordered to use nothing but bayonets. Only when they breached the earthworks did they make themselves known, shouting, "The fort's our own!" The brilliance of the plan was evident in the speed of victory: Stony Point was taken within the hour. It's been lauded as "the boldest venture of the war."

The Battle of Stony Point by Rufus Zogbaum, courtesy West Point Museum. Right: Revolutionary War encampment of the Brigade of the American Revolution, Stony Point.

Taking away more than 500 prisoners, the Americans quickly abandoned the fort – they didn't have the troops to garrison both West Point and Stony Point. Still, the victory had its desired effect, boosting morale in the ranks and throughout the colonies. It even impressed the enemy. "The rebels made the attack with bravery they never before exhibited," wrote British Commodore George Collier.

"His Excellency took out his spectacles, observing that he had grown gray in their service, and now found himself going blind."

First in war: An on-the-scene account of General Washington's address to his officers, from *The Life and Journals of Major Samuel Shaw* (1847)

The meeting of the officers was in itself exceedingly respectable, the matters they were called to deliberate upon were of the most serious nature, and the unexpected attendance of the Commander-in-chief heightened the solemnity of the scene. Every eye was fixed upon the illustrious man, and attention to their beloved general held the assembly mute. He opened the meeting by apologizing for his appearance there, which was by no means his intention when he published the order which directed them to assemble. But the diligence used in circulating the anonymous pieces rendered it necessary that he should give his sentiments to the army on the nature and tendency of them, and determined him to avail himself of the present opportunity; and, in order to do it with greater perspicuity, he had committed his thoughts to writing, which, with the indulgence of his brother officers, he would take the liberty of reading to them... One circumstance in reading this letter must not be omitted. His Excellency, after reading the first paragraph, made a short pause, took out his spectacles, and begged the indulgence of his audience while he put them on, observing at the same time, that he had grown gray in their service, and now found himself growing blind. There was something so natural, so unaffected, in this appeal, as rendered it superior to the most studied oratory; it forced its way to the heart, and you might see sensibility moisten every eye...

I cannot dismiss this subject without observing that it is happy for America that she has a *patriot army*, and equally so that a *Washington* is its leader. I rejoice in the opportunities I have had of seeing this great man in a variety of situations;– calm and intrepid where the battle raged, patient and persevering under the pressure of misfortune, moderate and possessing himself in the full career of victory. Great as these qualifications deservedly render him, he never appeared to me more truly so than at the assembly we have been speaking of. On other occasions he has been supported by the exertions of an army and the countenance of his friends; but in this he stood single and alone. There was no saying where the passions of an army, which were not a little inflamed, might lead; but it was generally allowed that longer forebearance was dangerous, and moderation had ceased to be a virtue. Under these circumstances he appeared, not at the head of his troops, but as it were in opposition to them; and for a dreadful moment the interests of the army and its General seemed to be in competition! He spoke,– every doubt was dispelled, and the tide of patriotism rolled again in its wonted course. Illustrious man! What he says of the army may with equal justice be applied to his own character. "Had this day been wanting, the world had never seen the last stage of perfection to which human nature is capable of attaining."

George Washington had vanquished the British. Now a threat appeared from within his own ranks.

After the Americans' victory at Yorktown, Virginia, in October 1781, the fighting came to a close, but the Continental Army couldn't disband until an official cease-fire was declared. As negotiations dragged on into 1782, the troops settled at New Windsor, within striking distance of Britain's last stronghold in Manhattan. The 7,500 men (along with 500 wives and children) constructed a virtual village, erecting more than 600 log huts arrayed in neat rows. They'd remain there until April 1783. (Today, the grounds are a state historic site.)

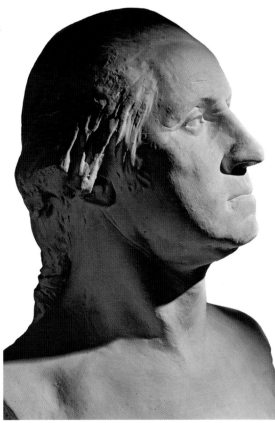

Portrait bust of George Washington. Left: Washington's Headquarters, Newburgh.

While the rank and file at the New Windsor Cantonment occasionally griped, some officers did worse: They plotted a coup. Fed up with the cavalier attitude of Congress toward them – especially the handling of their pay – the men considered establishing a military dictatorship after the war. They expressed this threat in two anonymous letters, known as the Newburgh Addresses, which they sent to Congress.

Headquartered at the Jonathan Hasbrouck house in nearby Newburgh – his home for more time during the war than anywhere else – Washington knew he had to nip this homegrown revolt in the bud. To him, the thought of anything but a democracy for the states was anathema. Already he'd quashed a suggestion that he be crowned king of the new nation.

At a regular meeting of officers at the cantonment on March 15, 1783, the commander made a dramatic, unexpected appearance. He pledged to do what he could for his unpaid men, begging them to desist from destroying what they had fought so hard to achieve. His prepared address is little remembered. It was an extemporaneous remark – Washington speaking directly from the heart, with self-deprecating humor about his eyesight – that convinced the officers to support Congress. His one-sentence throwaway line may have saved the nation.

"I am convinced that this is the safest course for your liberty, your dignity, and your happiness."

Arguments for a strong national government: Alexander Hamilton's "The Federalist, No. 1," the first of 85 convincing essays (1787)

To the People of the State of New York:

AFTER an unequivocal experience of the inefficiency of the subsisting federal government, you are called upon to deliberate on a new Constitution for the United States of America. The subject speaks its own importance; comprehending in its consequences nothing less than the existence of the UNION, the safety and welfare of the parts of which it is composed, the fate of an empire in many respects the most interesting in the world. It has been frequently remarked that it seems to have been reserved to the people of this country, by their conduct and example, to decide the important question, whether societies of men are really capable or not of establishing good government from reflection and choice, or whether they are forever destined to depend for their political constitutions on accident and force. If there be any truth in the remark, the crisis at which we are arrived may with propriety be regarded as the era in which that decision is to be made; and a wrong election of the part we shall act may, in this view, deserve to be considered as the general misfortune of mankind...

An enlightened zeal for the energy and efficiency of government will be stigmatized as the offspring of a temper fond of despotic power and hostile to the principles of liberty. An over-scrupulous jealousy of danger to the rights of the people, which is more commonly the fault of the head than of the heart, will be represented as mere pretence and artifice, the stale bait for popularity at the expense of the public good. It will not be forgotten, on the one hand, that jealousy is the usual concomitant of love, and that the noble enthusiasm of liberty is apt to be infected with a spirit of narrow and illiberal distrust. On the other hand, it will be equally forgotten that the vigor of government is essential to the security of liberty... History will teach us that of those men who have overturned the liberties of republics, the greatest number have begun their career by paying an obsequious court to the people, commencing as demagogues, and ending tyrants.

I have had an eye...to putting you upon your guard against all attempts, from whatever quarter, to influence your decision in a matter of the utmost moment to your welfare, by an impression other than those which may result from the evidence of truth. You will, no doubt, at the same time, have collected from the general scope of them, that they proceed from a source not unfriendly to the new Constitution. Yes, my countrymen, I owe to you that, after having given it an attentive consideration, I am clearly of opinion it is your interest to adopt it. I am convinced that this is the safest course for your liberty, your dignity, and your happiness...

Alexander Hamilton – the face on the $10 bill and the "architect" of the U.S. Constitution – was America's first great immigrant success story.

None of the Founding Fathers had more drive, or further to rise. Born illegitimately on the Caribbean island of Nevis and orphaned at age 12, young Alexander survived as a store clerk. A business whiz, his bosses sent him to America to get an education. He studied at King's College, today Columbia University. When the Revolution broke out, he formed his own artillery company, then landed the plum as General Washington's aide-de-camp. Later, he served as the nation's first treasury secretary (hence his banknote portrait) and helped found two Manhattan institutions: the Bank of New York and the *New York Post*. He even bagged a trophy wife, becoming son-in-law of Philip Schuyler, one of Albany's leading (and richest) citizens.

But nothing better exemplifies Hamilton's zeal than his efforts to create the United States. As early as 1780, he espoused the need for a strong national government with broad powers over the individually weaker states. It would take seven years for anyone to act on his suggestion.

Nine states quickly ratified the new constitution Hamilton had helped draft in Philadelphia in 1787. That was enough to make it the supreme law of the land, supplanting the ineffective Articles of Confederation. But without the backing of Virginia and Hamilton's New York, it was worthless.

With James Madison and John Jay, he wrote *The Federalist* papers, essays defending the constitution. They became required reading in local newspapers, but

Portrait of first Treasury Secretary Alexander Hamilton on $10 bill. Left: Memorial to Hamilton at Weehawken, New Jersey, dueling site where he was mortally wounded by Vice President Aaron Burr. The Manhattan skyline is in the background.

at New York's ratification convention in Poughkeepsie, the anti-Federalists held a big majority. With his skillful oratory and outright pleading, Hamilton turned the tide. On July 26, 1788, the convention's Federalists squeaked to a three-vote victory. Virginia was already on board. A testament to Hamilton's foresight – and the strength of the government he helped frame – the United States is today the world's longest-surviving democratic republic.

Had Hamilton not been mortally wounded in an 1804 duel with U.S. Vice President Aaron Burr, who knows what more he might have accomplished? But one thing is certain: He would never have been America's commander in chief. The constitution he fought for prohibits foreign-born citizens from serving as president.

"With an heart full of love and gratitude, I now take leave of you. I most devoutly wish that your latter days may be as prosperous and happy as your former ones have been glorious and honorable." – General George Washington's farewell to his officers (1783)

Praising God: From President Washington's first inaugural address (1789)

Such being the impressions under which I have, in obedience to the public summons, repaired to the present station, it would be peculiarly improper to omit in this first official act my fervent supplications to that Almighty Being who rules over the universe, who presides in the councils of nations, and whose providential aids can supply every human defect, that His benediction may consecrate to the liberties and happiness of the people of the United States a Government instituted by themselves for these essential purposes, and may enable every instrument employed in its administration to execute with success the functions allotted to his charge… No people can be bound to acknowledge and adore the Invisible Hand which conducts the affairs of men more than those of the United States. Every step by which they have advanced to the character of an independent nation seems to have been distinguished by some token of providential agency; and in the important revolution just accomplished in the system of their united government the tranquil deliberations and voluntary consent of so many distinct communities from which the event has resulted can not be compared with the means by which most governments have been established without some return of pious gratitude, along with an humble anticipation of the future blessings which the past seem to presage… You will join with me, I trust, in thinking that there are none under the influence of which the proceedings of a new and free government can more auspiciously commence…

And blessing good government: From a letter to the Count de Moustier (1790)

A short relaxation from public business, and an indulgence in the pleasures of country life during the recess of Congress, have greatly contributed to improve my health, which is now, thank God, perfectly reestablished. From the interest you take in the prosperity of the United States, you will learn with pleasure, that their happiness continues to advance, and that there is great reason to conclude it will be lasting. The wisdom and integrity, manifested in the measures of Congress, have secured to them the confidence of their constituents, and the respect of our domestic neighbours; with the most considerable of whom, treaties, dictated by justice and national generosity, have been concluded and will, in all probability, be faithfully maintained. The aggregate happiness of society, which is best promoted by the practice of a virtuous policy, is, or ought to be, the end of all government. Such, I am happy in telling you, appears to be the object of our legislative regulations….

President Washington kisses the Bible at his first inauguration, 1789. Left: Embroidery of General Washington's triumphal entry into New York City, 1783.

As commander in chief, George Washington bid adieu to his fellow Continental officers at Manhattan's Fraunces Tavern on December 4, 1783. He intended to enjoy his twilight years as a gentleman farmer at Mount Vernon. Six years later, he was back in the city, as president of the United States. An even heavier burden now rested upon his shoulders.

Washington's comrades, looking at his careworn face, commented on the toll his service to the nation had taken. Yet when it came time to elect the republic's first leader under its new constitution, he had been the unanimous choice. Reflecting on the daunting prospect of the job, he likened himself to "a culprit who is going to the place of his execution." Unable to say no to the people, he undertook his pioneering presidency with humility.

Arriving in Manhattan, the country's temporary capital, Washington found Congress already engaged in politics as usual. He cooled his heels for a week while statesmen haggled over protocol for his investiture. Finally, on April 30, 1789, he stood on the balcony of Federal Hall at Broad and Wall Streets and intoned the Oath of Office administered by New York's Chancellor Robert Livingston. A staunch patriot, Livingston's riverfront home (Clermont, now a state historic site) had been burned by the British in 1777. Standing before Washington, he must have felt sweet revenge. The intent of the Declaration of Independence, which he helped draft, was now fulfilled through the inauguration of a constitutional government presided over by a president.

As he had during the Revolution, President Washington refused to accept his $25,000 annual salary, which no doubt burdened his wife's efforts to maintain an official household. (He did receive an unchallenged expense account.) Yet First Lady Martha Washington never once complained about her husband's devotion to the United States – or his frequent absences. "I cannot blame him for having acted according to his ideas of duty in obeying the voice of his country," she wrote. Behind the Father of our Country was a devoted Mother.

Spring

Preceding pages: Mountain laurel at Lake Minnewaska, atop the Shawangunk Mountains.

Above: Springtime invites a day's end workout in Manhattan's Riverside Park.

Windsurfer off Little Stony Point, Hudson Highlands.

Many stately mansions with elegant gardens, once private pleasure grounds, are now publicly maintained as house museums (see tourism guide on page 140). Lyndhurst (left), the Gothic-inspired country estate once home to Wall Street tycoon Jay Gould, is now a National Trust property in Tarrytown. Poughkeepsie's Locust Grove, the Tuscan-style villa of Samuel F.B. Morse, is supported by a local nonprofit organization. The site's visitor center explores the creativity of this "American Leonardo," famous for both his fine paintings and telegraphic inventions. Both houses were designed by Alexander Jackson Davis, the Hudson Valley's preeminent 19th-century architect.

Leaf pop – amber and chartreuse herald springtime in valley forests.

Overleaf: Fishermen net shad on the Tappan Zee (Ted Spiegel photograph © *National Geographic Magazine*).

Gardeners expand nature's palette with yellows and reds at Crescent Garden in Manhattan's Fort Tryon Park (left).
A Henry Moore sculpture accents the "golden mile" pathway through PepsiCo's Donald M. Kendall Sculpture Garden in Purchase.

Seasonal events demonstrating crafts and tasks of the past get people involved. Draft horses are put through their paces at the state's Stony Kill Farm Environmental Education Center in Wappingers Falls. Quilting techniques are displayed at Historic Hudson Valley's Van Cortlandt Manor.

Within their borders, Hudson Valley gardeners orchestrate a marvelous springtime blooming season. They cultivate plants of myriad textures and colors, supplying delight-filled eye candy. In the arboretum of Northeast conifers at Albany's Academy Park, each species has a distinct branch and needle pattern. At nearby Washington Park, tens of thousands of flowering bulbs salute Albany's Dutch heritage during the annual Tulip Festival in May.

Fishermen at Newburgh display prize-winning striped bass. Left: Student chefs at the Culinary Institute of America in Hyde Park offer a sampling of their American Bounty Restaurant menu – salad, soup, lamb, and apple crisp – prepared under the watchful eye of their instructors.

The 19th Century

"I feel infinitely more pleasure in reflecting on the immense advantage that my country will derive from the invention."

Wags called it a "tea kettle on a raft," a "backwoods sawmill mounted on a scow," and "Fulton's folly." But when the *North River Steamboat* began its maiden voyage to Albany on August 17, 1807, Robert Fulton enjoyed the last laugh.

Fulton seemed an unlikely man to be ending the wind's dominance over Hudson River travel. He was trained as a portrait painter, but he was also a mechanical genius who perfected two staples of 20th-century warfare, the submarine and torpedo. More important, he fervently believed in the potential of machines. While he didn't invent the steamboat, he was the first to make it practical and profitable.

His 146-foot boat – popularly called the *Clermont*, after the home of Fulton's business partner, Chancellor Robert Livingston – chugged at a steady four-and-a-half miles an hour, the steam to turn its paddlewheel generated by a coal-fired copper boiler. The trip to Albany was completed in 32 hours. People were so afraid the craft would explode that Fulton found only two passengers – a couple of Frenchmen – willing to pay the $3 fare for the return voyage to Manhattan.

Soon, however, steamboats were commonplace on all rivers and oceans. (Wisely, Livingston had secured for the partners a 20-year monopoly for steam traffic on New York waters. The U.S. Supreme Court put an end to their transportation domination in 1824.) By 1850, more than 150 steamers were churning up the Hudson alone, carrying a million passengers annually. Some were equipped with accommodations rivaling the finest hotels.

Night boat on the Hudson, 1871.
Left: *The Clermont* by Samuel Ward Stanton, courtesy Joan Stickley.

Fulton's vital contribution to the valley – and to the revolutionizing of transportation – was recognized when festivities were held in 1909 to mark both the centennial of his maiden trip and the tricentennial of Henry Hudson's voyage. "We celebrate in Hudson the great race of men who made the age of discovery," reads the official account. "We celebrate in Fulton the great race of men whose inventive genius has laid the foundation for a broader, nobler and more permanent civilization the world over."

Tea kettle on a raft:
Robert Fulton relates the success of his maiden Hudson River steamboat voyage to friend Joel Barlow (1807)

My steamboat voyage to Albany and back has turned out rather more favorably than I had calculated. The distance from New York to Albany is one hundred and fifty miles. I ran it up in thirty-two hours, and down in thirty. I had a light breeze against me the whole way, both going and coming, and the voyage has been performed wholly by the power of the steam engine. I overtook many sloops and schooners, beating to the windward, and parted with them as if they had been at anchor. The power of propelling boats by steam is now fully proved.

The morning I left New York, there were not perhaps thirty persons in the city who believed that the boat would ever move one mile an hour, or be of the least utility, and while we were putting off from the wharf, which was crowded with spectators, I heard a number of sarcastic remarks. This is the way in which ignorant men compliment what they call philosophers and projectors. Having employed much time, money and zeal in accomplishing this work, it gives me, as it will you, great pleasure to see it fully answer my expectations. It will give a cheap and quick conveyance to the merchandize on the Mississippi, Missouri, and other great rivers, which are now laying open their treasures to the enterprise of our countrymen; and although the prospect of personal emolument has been some inducement to me, yet I feel infinitely more pleasure in reflecting on the immense advantage that my country will derive from the invention.

An "admirable invention" – British actress Fanny Kemble reports on her Hudson River steamboat excursion (1832)

Nobody who has not seen it, can conceive the strange aspect of the long room on one of these fine boats at meal-time. The crowd, the hurry, the confusion of tongues, like the sound of many waters, the enormous consumption of eatables, the mingled demands for more, the cloud of black waiters hovering down the sides of the immense tables, the hungry, eager faces seated at them, form altogether a most amusing subject of contemplation, and a caricaturist would find ample matter for his vein in almost every other devouring countenance. As far as regards the speed, safety, and convenience with which these vessels enable one to perform what would be in any other conveyance most fatiguing journeys, they are admirable inventions. The way in which they are conducted, too, deserves, the highest commendation. Nothing can exceed the comfort with which they are fitted up, the skill with which they are managed, and the order and alacrity with which passengers are taken up from, or landed at the various points along the river.

CADET LIFE AT WEST POINT.—Sketched by Theodore R. Davis.—[See Page 426.]

"Thayer's insistence on leadership integrated by excellence in both character and knowledge has been the cornerstone of the West Point Experience."

As any 19th-century traveler could have told you, West Point is a place of superlatives. It's the nation's longest continuously occupied military garrison (soldiers arrived in 1778). The U.S. Military Academy, founded there in 1802, was America's first engineering school. Its military museum, opened in 1854, is the Western Hemisphere's largest. Visitors can witness the valley's grandest spectacles – a cadet dress parade or a performance by the academy band, the nation's oldest musical group. And the scenery? Incomparable.

General George Washington, who'd relied on European engineers during the Revolution, noted the need for a school to train military experts in 1796. "If we desire to secure peace," he said, "it must be known that we are...ready for war." The academy didn't become a first-rate university until Colonel Sylvanus Thayer was named superintendent in 1817. He demanded that cadets recite "in every subject every day," meaning they had to know the material *before* class. Thanks to the rigorous instruction, academy grads – the first civil engineers formally

Colonel Sylvanus Thayer, courtesy West Point Museum. Left: *Cadet Life at West Point*, circa 1870, courtesy Special Collections, U.S.M.A. Library. Over 4,000 cadets learn and train at the academy today.

trained in America – took the lead in surveying new rail lines, designing forts and harbors, developing roads and aqueducts. Brown University President Francis Wayland noted in 1850 that West Point did more "to build up the system of internal improvements in the United States" than the rest of the nation's 120 colleges combined.

Cadets also learned a thing or two about leading armies. In 55 of 60 major Civil War battles, both sides were commanded by men following their West Point play books, including Grant and Lee. Two notable 19th-century academy dropouts: Edgar Allan Poe and James McNeill Whistler.

No 19th-century American Grand Tour was complete without stepping upon West Point's plain, to witness military drills and view the Hudson Highlands. "The beauty and wild sublimity of what I beheld seemed almost to crush my faculties," wrote an English visitor in 1832. "Though I were to live a thousand years, I never can forget it."

Sylvanus Thayer comes to West Point's rescue, from *Bugle Notes*, the cadet handbook

Reporting at West Point in July 1817, [Colonel Sylvanus] Thayer found most cadets absent or on special leave, regulations disregarded, studies inadequately mastered, and the Academy in a state of disorganization. Thayer approached the problem of administering the Military Academy with two guiding principles in mind. The first principle which he insisted upon making effective was strict adherence to the rule of discipline and subordination. Supporting fundamentals which had to be fostered at the Military Academy, he felt, were an ardent attachment to the military profession, a reasonable desire for advancement and a strong and dignified regard for personal reputation.

A second principle guiding Thayer was the advancement or promotion according to merit, with no distinction between students because of financial or family background. The West Point teaching staff accepted these principles as their own, and joined Thayer in their application to the day-to-day administration of the Academy....

His innovations in educational methods ensured that the cadets not only learned but retained their subjects. Basically, he demanded that the cadets develop habits of mental discipline and maintain standards of scholarship that have grown in importance through the years. He emphasized habits of regular study and laid down a rule that every cadet had to pass every course to graduate.... Thayer's insistence on leadership integrated by excellence in both character and knowledge has been the cornerstone of the West Point Experience since his day. Ralph Waldo Emerson, visiting West Point in 1863, spoke of the "air of probity, or veracity, and of loyalty" the cadets had; and when, in 1898, the present coat of arms was adopted, the motto of "Duty, Honor, Country" was but a later generation's attempt to put Thayer's ideals into words.

Cadet Jacob Bailey describes the routine – and considers his future (1832)

I thought when I entered the first class [fourth year] that we should have a comparatively easy time, but the contrary was the case, as we have been obliged to study this year, almost as hard as when Lacroix' Algebra was our trouble. I have had so much writing to do, that I am heartily tired out. Memoir after memoir, and note after note, have been required of us, ever since last September....

We shall [have] a very busy time between now and next June, it will take about a week to examine my class, next June we shall have so many subjects to be called upon, Civil engineering I shall pay the most attention. The number of Railroads constructing in all parts of our country will furnish employment for many engineers....

General Winfield Scott's "fixed opinion" (1860), which every cadet must memorize

I give it as my fixed opinion, that but for our graduated cadets, the war between the United States and Mexico might, and probably would have lasted some four or five years, with, in its first half, more defeats than victories falling to our share; whereas, in less than two campaigns, we conquered a great country and a peace without the loss of a single battle or skirmish.

Many of the officers Scott commanded in Mexico would square off against each other in the Civil War.

"How many manufacturing establishments have had the value of every thing connected with them doubled by this meeting of the waters!"

New York Harbor celebration of the Erie Canal's completion, 1825. Right: The Erie Canal, circa 1825. Both courtesy Special Collections, U.S.M.A. Library.

Four feet of water and a mess of mules. That's all it took to turn the Hudson River into America's first superhighway and New York into its richest city. Hee-haw for the Erie Canal!

Plans for a canal to the west were nothing new – as early as the 1770s, Royal Governor William Tryon had proposed one – but New York Governor De Witt Clinton had the clout to make it happen. Work on the waterway, initially derided as "Clinton's big ditch," began in 1817. Eight years, 363 miles, and $7.5 million later, it was completed. Forty feet wide and four feet deep, the redubbed "Eighth Wonder of the World" featured 83 locks to carry the canal down the 568-foot elevation drop between Lake Erie and the Hudson River. The dirty work had been done by predominantly Irish laborers who earned 80 cents a day for 12 hours of digging. Amazingly, not a single professional engineer had a hand in the planning and design.

It didn't take long for the canal to prove its worth. Within a year, mules were pulling 2,000 boats along it. Before, it cost $120 a ton for cargo to be shipped from Buffalo to New York; now, the price was $4. Travel time was cut in half, from 20 days to ten. By 1835, the state had recouped every cent of the construction costs.

Clinton had vowed that the Erie Canal would make Manhattan "the greatest emporium in the world." That promise was fulfilled: The city's wharves became the central depot for agricultural goods from the Midwest, cotton from the South, and manufactured items from New England. In 1828, customs duties collected at the port paid all of the federal government's day-to-day expenses. By 1874, 60 percent of U.S. exports passed through Manhattan's harbor on their way to points around the world.

William Stone's official account of the ceremony at the mouth of the Hudson River marking the completion of the Erie Canal (November 4, 1825)

The boats were...formed in a circle.... His Excellency Governor Clinton then proceeded to perform the ceremony of commingling the waters of the Lakes with the Ocean, by pouring a keg of that of Lake Erie into the Atlantic; upon which he delivered the following Address—

"This solemnity, at this place, on the first arrival of vessels from Lake Erie, is intended to indicate and commemorate the navigable communication, which has been accomplished between our Mediterranean Seas and the Atlantic Ocean, in about eight years, to the extent of more than four hundred and twenty-five miles, by the wisdom, public spirit, and energy of the people of the state of New York; and may God of the Heavens and the Earth smile most propitiously on this work, and render it subservient to the best interests of the human race."

Thus has closed one of the greatest, happiest, proudest, most propitious scenes, our state has ever witnessed... What visions of glory rush upon the mind, as it attempts to lift the curtain of futurity and survey the rising destiny of New York through the long vista of years to come! For, whatever party rules, whatever political chief rises or falls, agriculture, manufactures and commerce, must still remain the greatest of our concerns; and by the opening of the Canal, these three great vital interests are all most eminently promoted. What a wide spread region of cultivated soil has already been brought within the near vicinity of the greatest market on our continent! How many manufacturing establishments have had the value of every thing connected with them doubled by this "meeting of the waters!" How vastly have the internal resources of this metropolis been in one day practically extended!

The authors and builders – the heads who planned, and the hands who executed this stupendous work, deserve a perennial monument; and they will have it. To borrow an expression from the highest of all sources, "the works which they have done, these will bear witness of them." Europe begins already to admire – America can never forget to acknowledge, that THEY HAVE BUILT THE LONGEST CANAL IN THE WORLD IN THE LEAST TIME, WITH THE LEAST EXPERIENCE, FOR THE LEAST MONEY, AND TO THE GREATEST PUBLIC BENEFIT.

I've got a mule, and her name is Sal.

Fifteen miles on the Erie Canal.

She's a good old worker and a good old pal.

Fifteen miles on the Erie Canal.

We've hauled some barges in our day,

Filled with lumber, coal, and hay,

And we know ev'ry inch of the way

From Albany to Buffalo.

Low bridge! Everybody down!

Low bridge, 'cause we're coming to a town;

And you'll always know your neighbor,

You'll always know your pal,

If you've ever navigated on the Erie Canal.

"We sons of patriot sires, now swear—Your loads we will no longer bear"

Outfitted in gaily colored costumes, their faces hidden behind gruesome sheepskin masks, and tooting tin horns, the "Indians" of the upper Hudson Valley went on the warpath in the 1840s.

Beneath these getups were tenant farmers rebelling against the 200-year-old patroon system that rendered them virtual serfs to land-owning families like the Van Rensselaers and Livingstons, to whom, in addition to rent, they were forced to pay yearly tribute in produce. There were thousands of them, many descendants of the original settlers who had cleared the land for the first Lords of the Manor (see page 21). These farmers didn't expect a free ride: They wanted to *buy* their land. And they didn't mince words. "It is foul, cruel, and oppressive to protect and encourage a lazy, worthless, immoral, and bastard aristocracy to ride roughshod over the pith and marrow of the country, the laborious husbandman," one of them said.

The Anti-Rent War began in 1839, after the death of Stephen Van Rensselaer, lord of the 40-square-mile Manor of Rensselaerswyck. When his heirs tried to collect unpaid rents, mobs prevented sheriffs from evicting those unable to come up with the money. The insurrection quickly spread to 160,000-acre Livingston Manor. By and large, it was a nonviolent affair: The distant sound of a tin horn was enough to send most lawmen scurrying. The farmers resorted to speech-making and song to share their plight with the wider public. Eventually, their message reached Albany. Under the revised state constitution of 1846, future long-term leases were abolished. And thanks to the fear instilled by the rent-protesting mobs of calico-clad "Indians," the manor lords had begun selling off their land. Henceforth, even the lowliest valley farmer could be king of his castle.

Attack on the sheriff of Albany by disguised farmers, courtesy Bettman/Corbis. **Left: A farm on Catskill Creek.**

Tales of the Anti-Rent War in broadside…

ANTIRENTERS! AWAKE! AROUSE!

Let the opponents of Patroonery rally in their strength.
A great crisis is approaching. Now is the time to strike.
The minions of Patroonery are at work.
Arouse! Awake!
And
Strike till the last armed foe expires
Strike for your altars and your fires,
Strike for the green graves of your sires,
God and your happy homes!

…and song

Our feudal lords in coaches ride,
Puffed up with vanity and pride,
Their boasted wealth, they do forget,
Was purchased by the tenants' sweat.

Proud haughty barons—ye may spy
The tempest gathering in the sky—
The storm ye once thought would not last,
Ye may discern has not yet passed.

We sons of patriot sires, now swear—
Your loads we will no longer bear;
A thousand hearts now beat as one,
To finish what we have begun.

But shout, brothers, shout!
Oh, shout, brothers, shout!
Loud sound the horn
Upon the morn
Of Independence Day!

"Day by day and year by year I've toil'd
To grasp your beauty; but I have been foil'd."

Kaaterskill Falls by Thomas Cole (1826), courtesy The Westervelt-Warner Museum of American Art. Right: _Clouds over Olana_ (1872), oil sketch on paper by Frederic Church; courtesy New York State Department of Parks, Recreation and Historic Preservation.

A Painter – by Thomas Cole

I know 'tis vain ye mountains, and ye woods
To strive to match your wild, and wonderous hues,
Ye rocks and lakes, and ever rolling floods,
The gold-cinctur'd eve, or morn begemm'd with dews –

Yes, day by day and year by year I've toil'd
In the lone chamber, and the sunny field
To grasp your beauty; but I have been foil'd
I cannot conquer; but I will not yield –

How oft have I, where spread the pictur'd scene
Wrought on the canvas with fond, anxious care,
Deemed I had equaled nature's forests green,
Her lakes, her rock, and e'en the ambient air.

Vain unpious thought! such feverish fancies sweep
Swift from the brain – when nature's landscapes break
Upon the thrilling sense – O I could weep
Not that she is so beautiful; but I so weak –

O! for a power to snatch the living light
From heaven, and darkness from some deep abyss,
Made palpable: with skill to mingle right
Their mystery of beauty! Then mine would be bliss!

America's fling with the Romantic Movement began in the Hudson Valley.

It started with Thomas Cole. An English émigré artist based in Manhattan, he took frequent sketching trips to the Catskill Mountains, where he was entranced by their rugged beauty. Back in his studio, he created canvases in an exciting new manner. Breaking away from the rigidity of portraiture, which required the artist to duplicate faithfully all he saw, Cole crafted imaginary landscapes that explored nature's untamed majesty and its temporal qualities. Manipulating light and shade, these highly personal paintings captured moods, from joy to desolation. It was the first American art that made the viewer "feel" – the essence of Romantic art.

Cole's first three Catskills canvases, painted in 1825, were instant hits, earning him $25 apiece. (Today, they sell in the millions.) As other painters headed to the hills for inspiration, he was recognized as the founder of the Hudson River School, America's first homegrown art movement. The depictions of mountain sunsets and shady glades created by Cole and his 100 or so followers served as unwitting advertisements for the Catskills' burgeoning resorts. One historian even claims Cole is responsible for the great American migration to the suburbs. Cole himself eventually left Manhattan for the river town of Catskill. From the porch of his house, dubbed Cedar Grove, he could see the mountains he'd made famous.

While Cole daubed paint, Andrew Jackson Downing fashioned artistry out of the valley's rocks and trees. The self-taught son of a Newburgh nurseryman, America's first great landscape architect forsook geometric gardens for the "Picturesque," which he defined as "a certain spirited irregularity." Downing's designs so perfectly complemented the valley's natural beauty that it was hard to distinguish his landscapes from God's. The confusion was intentional.

He suggested his clients build houses matching their Romantic surroundings – Swiss chalets, Italianate villas, Gothic fancies. And he was an ardent environmentalist. "If we have neither old castles nor old associations," he wrote, "we have at least…old trees that can teach us lessons of antiquity, not less instructive and poetical than the ruins of a past age."

Sadly, little of Downing's work survives. But a grand Romantic landscape still exists at Olana, the self-designed estate of Cole's most esteemed pupil, Frederic Edwin Church (see pages 152-3). He considered Olana's grounds his artistic masterpiece. "I can make more and better landscapes in this way than tampering with canvas and paint," he said.

JEC Aug · 1872

The Ride of the Headless Horseman: From Washington Irving's "The Legend of Sleepy Hollow"

All the stories of ghosts and goblins that [Ichabod Crane] had heard in the afternoon, now came crowding upon his recollection. The night grew darker and darker; the stars seemed to sink deeper in the sky, and driving clouds occasionally hid them from his sight. He had never felt so lonely and dismal. He was, moreover, approaching the very place where many of the scenes of the ghost stories had been laid. In the center of the road stood an enormous tulip-tree, which towered like a giant above all the other trees of the neighborhood, and formed a kind of landmark. Its limbs were gnarled and fantastic, large enough to form trunks for ordinary trees, twisting down almost to the earth, and rising again into the air. It was connected with the tragical story of the unfortunate André, who had been taken prisoner hard by; and was universally known by the name of Major André's tree. [John André was subsequently hanged for serving as the British liaison enabling Benedict Arnold's treason.] The common people regarded it with a mixture of respect and superstition, partly out of sympathy for the fate of the ill-starred namesake, and partly from the tales of strange sights and doleful lamentations told concerning it.

As Ichabod approached this fearful tree, he began to whistle; he thought his whistle was answered—it was but a blast sweeping sharply through the dry branches. As he approached a little nearer, he though he saw something white hanging in the midst of the tree—he paused and ceased whistling; but on looking more narrowly, perceived that it was a place where the tree had been scathed by lightning, and the white wood laid bare. Suddenly he heard a groan—his teeth chattered and his knees smote against the saddle; it was but the rubbing of one huge bough upon another, as they were swayed about by the breeze. He passed the tree in safety, but new perils lay before him.

About two hundred yards from the tree a small brook crossed the road, and ran into a marshy and thickly-wooded glen, known by the name of Wiley's swamp. A few rough logs, laid side by side, served for a bridge over this stream. On that side of the road where the brook entered the wood, a group of oaks and chestnuts, matted thick with wild grape-vines, threw a cavernous gloom over it. To pass this bridge was the severest trial. It was at this identical spot that the unfortunate André was captured, and under covert of those chestnuts and vines were the sturdy yeoman concealed who surprised him. This has ever been considered a haunted stream, and fearful are the feelings of the schoolboy who has to pass it alone after dark.

As he approached the stream his heart began to thump; he summoned up, however, all his resolution, gave his horse half a score of kicks in the ribs, and attempted to dash briskly across the bridge; but instead of starting forward, the perverse old animal made a lateral movement, and ran broadside against the fence. Ichabod, whose fears increased with the delay, jerked the reins on the other side, and kicked lustily with the contrary foot; it was all in vain; his steed started,

it is true, but it was only to plunge to the opposite side of the road into a thicket of brambles and alder bushes. The schoolmaster now bestowed both whip and heel upon the starveling ribs of old Gunpowder, who dashed forward, snuffling and snorting, but came to a stand just by the bridge with suddenness that had nearly sent his rider sprawling over his head. Just at this moment a splashy tramp by the side of the bridge caught the sensitive ear of Ichabod. In the dark shadow of the grove, on the margin of the brook, he beheld something huge, misshapen, black, and towering. It stirred not, but seemed gathered up in the gloom, like some gigantic monster ready to spring upon the traveler.

The hair of the affrighted pedagogue rose upon his head with terror. What was to be done? To turn and fly was now too late; and besides, what chance was there of escaping ghost or goblin, if such it was, which could ride upon the wings of wind? Summoning up, therefore, a show of courage, he demanded in stammering accents—"Who are you?" He received no reply. He repeated his demand in a still more agitated voice. Still there was no answer. Once more he cudgeled the sides of the inflexible Gunpowder, and, shutting his eyes, broke forth with involuntary fervor into a psalm-tune. Just then the shadowy object of alarm put itself in motion, and, with a scramble and a bound, stood at once in the middle of the road. Though the night was dark and dismal, yet the form of the unknown might now in some degree be ascertained. He appeared to be a horseman of large dimensions, and mounted on a black horse of powerful frame. He made no offer of molestation or sociability, but kept aloof on one side of the road, jogging along on the blind side of old Gunpowder, who had now got over his fright and waywardness.

Ichabod, who had no relish for this strange midnight companion, and bethought himself of the adventure of Brom Bones with the Galloping Hessian, now quickened his steed, in hopes of leaving him behind. The stranger, however, quickened his horse to an equal pace. Ichabod pulled up, and fell into a walk, thinking to lag behind—the other did the same. His heart began to sink within him; he endeavored to resume his psalm-tune, but his parched tongue clove to the roof of his mouth, and he could not utter a stave. There was something in the moody and dogged silence of this pertinacious companion, that was mysterious and appalling. It was soon fearfully accounted for. On mounting a rising ground, which brought the figure of his fellow-traveller in relief against the sky, gigantic in height, and muffled in a cloak, Ichabod was horror-struck on perceiving that he was headless!—but his horror was still more increased, on observing that the head, which should have rested on his shoulders, was carried before him on the pommel of the saddle: his terror rose to desperation; he rained a shower of kicks and blows upon Gunpowder, hoping, by a sudden movement, to give his companion the slip—but the spectre started full jump with him. Away then they dashed, through thick and thin; stones flying, and sparks flashing at every bound. Ichabod's flimsy garments fluttered in the air, as he stretched his long lank body away over his horse's head, in the eagerness of his flight.

They had now reached the road which turns off to Sleepy Hollow; but

Gunpowder, who seemed possessed with a demon, instead of keeping up it, made an opposite turn, and plunged headlong down the hill to the left. This road leads through a sandy hollow, shaded by trees for about a quarter of a mile, where it crosses the bridge famous in goblin story, and just beyond swells the green knoll on which stands the whitewashed church.

As yet, the panic of the steed had given his unskillful rider an apparent advantage in the chase; but just as he had got half way through the hollow, the girths of the saddle gave way, and he felt it slipping from under him. He seized it by the pommel, and endeavored to hold it firm, but in vain; and had just time to save himself by clasping old Gunpowder round the neck, when the saddle fell to the earth, and he heard it trampled under foot by his pursuer. For a moment the terror of Hans Van Ripper's wrath passed across his mind—for it was his Sunday saddle; but this was no time for petty fears; the goblin was hard on his haunches; and (unskilled rider that he was!) he had much ado to maintain his seat; sometimes slipping on one side, sometimes on another, and sometimes jolted on the high ridge of his horse's backbone, with a violence that he verily feared would cleave him asunder.

An opening in the trees now cheered him with the hopes that the church bridge was at hand. The wavering reflection of a silver star in the bosom of the brook told him that he was not mistaken. He saw the walls of the church dimly glaring under the trees beyond. He recollected the place where Brom Bones's ghostly competitor had disappeared. "If I can but reach that bridge," thought Ichabod, "I am safe." Just then he heard the black steed panting and blowing close behind him; he even fancied that he felt his hot breath. Another convulsive kick in the ribs, and old Gunpowder sprang upon the bridge; he thundered over the resounding planks; he gained the opposite side; and now Ichabod cast a look behind, to see if his pursuer should vanish, according to rule, in a flash of fire and brimstone. Just then he saw the goblin rising in his stirrups, and in the very act of hurling his head at him, Ichabod endeavored to dodge the horrible missile, but too late. It encountered his cranium with a tremendous crash—he was tumbled headlong into the dust, and Gunpowder, the black steed, and the goblin rider, passed by like a whirlwind.

The next morning the old horse was found without his saddle, and with the bridle under his feet, soberly cropping the grass at his master's gate. Ichabod did not make his appearance at breakfast—dinner hour came, but no Ichabod. The boys assembled at the school-house, and strolled idly about the banks of the brook; but no schoolmaster. Hans Van Ripper now began to feel some uneasiness about the fate of poor Ichabod, and his saddle. An inquiry was set on foot, and after diligent investigation they came upon his traces. In one part of the road leading to the church was found the saddle trampled in the dirt; the tracks of horses' hoofs deeply dented in the road, and evidently at furious speed, were traced up to the bridge, beyond which, on the bank of a broad part of the brook, where the water ran deep and black, was found the hat of the unfortunate Ichabod, and close beside it a shattered pumpkin.

"I am always at a loss to know how much to believe of my own stories." – Author Washington Irving

Sunnyside, Washington Irving's home in Tarrytown. The wisteria was planted by Irving.

"A little old fashioned stone mansion, all made up of gable ends and as full of angles and corners as an old cocked hat." That's how Washington Irving described Sunnyside, his home in Tarrytown, about 30 miles north of Manhattan. The Hudson Valley's most famous writer purchased a simple 18th-century Dutch farmhouse and added a wealth of stylistic touches – Tudor chimneys, Dutch stepped gables, Gothic windows, a piazza, and a Spanish tower. Today, Sunnyside is one of a handful of house museums preserved and presented by Historic Hudson Valley.

Sunnyside was symbolic of the way Irving penned the vivid tales of Hudson Valley life that made him the first American author to achieve wealth and international renown. His characters were simple country folk, such as schoolteacher Ichabod Crane or ne'er-do-well Rip Van Winkle, around whom he wove fantastic tales involving headless horsemen, imps, and ghost ships. If the fabulous parts of his stories were not particularly original – much he cadged from German folk tales – the setting was. Irving's depictions of valley scenery made readers feel as if they were sailing through the craggy Highlands or tramping through a quiet Catskills glen.

Irving (1783-1859) and fellow valley resident James Fenimore Cooper were America's first Romantic writers, satisfying the public's craving for dramatic tales of the past. Cooper concentrated on derring-do along the 18th-century frontier. The Manhattan-born Irving focused on the region's Dutch connection. His first success, *A History of New York* (1809), written by the pseudonymous Diedrich Knickerbocker, offered a laugh-out-loud narrative of life under the infant colony's bumbling governors. One of literature's first historical fantasies, the work spawned many tales that have become part of valley folklore. Some of its "facts" later even found their way into serious histories.

That no doubt would have tickled Irving, who once admitted, "I am always at a loss to know how much to believe of my own stories."

"Harriet's outer clothes were torn from her, yet she never relinquished her hold of the man till she had dragged him to the river."

Free at last: Harriet Tubman rescues a slave – and causes a riot – in Troy. *From Harriet: Moses of her People* **by Sarah H. Bradford (1886)**

In the spring of 1860, Harriet Tubman was requested by [abolitionist] Mr. Gerrit Smith to go to Boston to attend a large anti-slavery meeting. On her way, she stopped at Troy to visit a cousin, and while there the colored people were one day startled with the intelligence that a fugitive slave…was already in the hands of the officers, and was to be taken back to the South. The instant Harriet heard the news, she started for the office of the United States Commissioner, scattering the tidings as she went. An excited crowd was gathered about the office, through which Harriet forced her way, and rushed up stairs to the door of the room where the fugitive was detained. A wagon was already waiting before the door to carry off the man, but the crowd was even then so great, and in such a state of excitement, that the officers did not dare to bring the man down… Time passed on, and he did not appear. "They've taken him out another way, depend upon that," said some of the colored people. "No," replied others, "there stands 'Moses' yet, and as long as she is there, he is safe." Harriet, now seeing the necessity for a tremendous effort for his rescue, sent out some little boys to cry fire. The bells rang, the crowd increased, till the whole street was a dense mass of people. Again and again the officers came out to try and clear the stairs…; others were driven down, but Harriet stood her ground… "Come, old woman, you must get out of this," said one of the officers; "If…you can't get down alone, some one will help you." Harriet, still putting on a greater appearance of decrepitude, twitched away from him, and kept her place. Offers were made to buy Charles from his master, who at first agreed to take twelve hundred dollars for him; but when this was subscribed, he immediately raised the price to fifteen hundred… At length the officers appeared, and announced to the crowd, that if they would open a lane to the wagon, they would promise to bring the man down the front way.

The lane was opened, and the man was brought out…with his wrists manacled together, walking between the U.S. Marshall and another officer… The moment they appeared, Harriet roused from her stooping posture, threw up a window, and cried to her friends: "Here he comes – take him!" and then darted down the stairs like a wild-cat. She seized one officer and pulled him down, then another, and tore him away from the man; and keeping her arms about the slave, she cried to her friends: "Drag us out! Drag him to the river!"… Again and again they were knocked down, the poor slave utterly helpless, with his manacled wrists, streaming with blood. Harriet's outer clothes were torn from her…yet she never relinquished her hold of the man, till she had dragged him to the river, where he was tumbled into a boat…

Costumed interpreters card wool at Philipsburg Manor (above) and craft barrels at Van Cortlandt Manor, Historic Hudson Valley.

The Underground Railroad chugged through the Hudson Valley. Ironically, this region that once depended on slaves was now sheltering them.

It's conveniently forgotten that New York was the largest slave-owning state north of the Mason-Dixon Line. The Netherlands had been engaged in the slave trade since the 1590s, so it's not surprising that ships bearing the human cargo appeared early on in New Netherland. The first 11 slaves arrived in 1625 to build roads and other infrastructure. By 1750, their number had swelled to 11,000 – 14 percent of the colony's population. Small farmers kept between one and five; large landowners, such as Frederick Philipse, owned more than 20. They were vital cogs in the burgeoning Hudson Valley economy. Finally, however, morals won out over money. The state began passing a series of emancipation laws in 1799, but slavery wasn't completely abolished in New York until 1827.

In 1850, the federal Fugitive Slave Law made it a crime to harbor escaped southern slaves. Valley residents came to the rescue, organizing a "line" on the Underground Railroad that shepherded them to safety in Canada. Traveling by night with the aid of "conductors," the African Americans hid by day in "stations" – crawl spaces, barns, and hidden passages. The secrecy of these stops was so zealously guarded that even today the true location of many Underground Railroad sites is impossible to determine.

Harriet Tubman, herself a former slave, was one of the most famous – and gutsiest – Underground Railroad conductors. This "American Moses" led more than 300 men and women to freedom through the Hudson Valley.

"Some have remarked that the Hudson Valley was the Silicon Valley of the 19th century."

The Industrial Revolution hit the Hudson Valley like a ton of homemade bricks and iron. Capital from New York City, combined with local ingenuity and an abundance of raw materials, fueled a manufacturing dynamo responsible for turning New York into the Empire State. Some have dubbed the region the Silicon Valley of the 19th century.

Troy was particularly known for its technological know-how, helped in part by hometown Rensselaer Polytechnic Institute, the country's second engineering school. (The U.S. Military Academy was the first.) The Burden Iron Works stamped most of the Union Army's horseshoes, while the Rensselaer Iron Works rolled the hull plates of the U.S. Navy's first ironclad ship, the *Monitor*. Troy's shirt, collar, and cuff factories employed 15,000 laborers, and it was said you couldn't go anywhere in the world without hearing the peal of a Meneely bell. Cotton weaving was king across the river in Cohoes. For a time, its 1,500-loom Harmony Mill was the country's longest factory.

Upstate didn't have a monopoly on innovative industry. Cold Spring's West Point Foundry turned out the engine for America's first locomotive; pipes for New York City's water system; and the Parrott gun, the rifled cannon credited with winning the Civil War. Its fame was far-flung: Jules Verne credits the foundry with manufacturing the spaceship-launching device in his classic novel *From the Earth to the Moon*.

The valley's raw materials supported America's building boom. Sing Sing Prison was opened atop a riverside quarry in 1824. Marble cut by its inmates adorned courthouses, churches, and the men's own cellblocks. A series of fires in Manhattan in the 1830s and '40s led to building codes requiring masonry construction. That was good news for valley brickworks. At the end of the 19th century, 130 lined the Hudson, all dependent on the

Buildings along Ossining's Crescent are constructed of locally fired bricks. **Right:** *The Gun Foundry* by John Ferguson Weir, courtesy Putnam County Historical Society & Foundry School Museum. The painting depicts Cold Spring's West Point Foundry.

region's enormous clay deposits. In Rosendale, a mother lode of limestone was turned into quick-setting cement used to erect the Brooklyn Bridge and the Statue of Liberty.

A good 19th-century rule of thumb: don't be surprised if *it* – whatever it is – was "Made in the Hudson Valley."

"The famous Hudson River scenery will eventually become a thing of the past."

"Crash!" "Boom!" These echoes of industry resounded through the Hudson Valley's most awe-inspiring landscapes, victims of America's 19th-century growth spurt.

Some railed against the despoliation of these natural treasures: "The ravages of the axe are daily increasing…oftentimes with a wantonness and barbarism scarcely credible in a civilized nation," wrote Thomas Cole in 1836. Yet for a long time theirs were voices crying in a quickly vanishing wilderness. In the Catskills, hemlock forests were decimated for the bark, needed to turn hides into leather. Upstate, lumbermen denuded the Adirondacks. And in the Palisades – the great curtain of rock that had wowed visitors since 1609 – 1,000 cubic yards was blasted daily to furnish gravel for new Manhattan streets.

Realizing it was now or never, the state began purchasing large tracts in the Catskills and Adirondacks in the early 1880s, creating forest preserves. In 1894, voters approved a "Forever Wild" amendment to the state constitution, guaranteeing the permanent protection of these lands. Originally covering 715,000 acres, the combined size of the two preserves has since quadrupled. In the Catskills, hikers now enjoy 300,000 acres of unspoiled wilderness.

The Palisades' tide turned after a galvanizing five-year campaign by the New Jersey Federation of Women's Clubs. The fact that ladies couldn't vote before 1920 didn't stop them from being among the valley's first – and staunchest – environmental activists. Their letter-writing campaigns and 1897 resolution demanding an end to the blasting eventually led to the formation in 1900 of the Palisades Interstate Park Commission, a unique cooperative venture between New York and New Jersey. (Spearheading the deal was New York's uber-environmentalist governor, Theodore Roosevelt; amazingly, he convinced his legislature to appropriate $400,000 to purchase land in New Jersey.) With financial help from titans like J.P. Morgan and John D. Rockefeller Jr., the quarrymen were bought out and the "booms" were banished. Today, nine million visitors enjoy more than 100,000 acres of Palisades Commission parkland stretching north from the George Washington Bridge to the Shawangunks.

The "Forever Wild" amendment to New York's constitution (1894)

The lands of the state, now owned or hereafter acquired, constituting the forest preserve as now fixed by law, shall be forever kept as wild forest lands. They shall not be leased, sold or exchanged, or be taken by any corporation, public or private, nor shall the timber thereon be sold, removed or destroyed.

Resolution to save the Palisades by the New Jersey Federation of Women's Clubs

The famous Hudson River scenery which the citizens of New Jersey hold in trust for all the world will eventually become a thing of the past to their lasting shame and disgrace. As it is, the glorious heritage of the people of the State is being trampled under the foot of man and beasts in the streets of Gotham. Will the State Federation realize its power for good in this matter?

New Jersey's protected Palisades. Left: The upper Hudson River in Adirondack State Park Preserve.

Summer

Two great summer gardens – the Cary Arboretum in Millbrook (above) and Kykuit, the Rockefeller Estate, at Pocantico Hills.

Preceding spread: Concertgoers celebrate summer at Clearwater's Great Hudson River Revival in Westchester County's Croton Point Park.
Singalongs reinforce dedication to continuing the renewal of the Hudson Valley's environment.

Color – both captured and fleeting – greets summer visitors at Beacon's Hudson Beach Glass and Poughkeepsie's Fourth of July riverfront festivities.

Summertime speeders – Thoroughbreds at Saratoga Springs' historic racetrack; outbound sailors from Rockland County's Nyack Boat Club.

Summertime students – Roping up at the base of the Shawangunk ridge, climbers learn technical skills needed to scale this world-class rock climbing challenge. Novice kayakers launching from Plum Point set out on a 20-mile paddle. A Hudson River Water Trail provides access to 65 launch points along the 158-mile sea-level passage from the Troy lock and dam to the tip of Manhattan.

Old-fashioned fun – whether making a splash in an Ulster County brook or taking to the sky at the Dutchess County Fair, Hudson Valley residents and visitors enjoy being "in the country."

Spectacular summer gathering places – Bethesda Fountain in Manhattan's Central Park and Trophy Point at the U.S. Military Academy, West Point. Both the people-watching on the plaza and the open-air concert by America's oldest professional band are free.

The 20th Century

"All of a sudden, I started life new, amongst people whose language I didn't understand."

For immigrants, America was the "golden door," as poet Emma Lazarus called it. At the dawn of the 20th century, that door burst wide open – and Ellis Island was the prime port of entry for the "huddled masses."

In the 19th century, residents of northern and central Europe – English, Irish, Scandinavian, and German – flocked to these shores; in the early 20th, it was the turn of wave after wave of eastern and southern Europeans – Italians, Poles, Greeks… Some 70 percent of all immigrants to reach America disembarked in Manhattan. Many followed in the footsteps of 15-year-old Annie Moore of County Cork, Ireland, the first person to pass through the portal of the federal "processing center" on New York Harbor's Ellis Island. From her arrival in 1892 until the onetime fortress closed in 1954, more than 12 million optimists waited and prayed for the okay to continue on to the mainland. Found lacking, some were returned to Europe. Many of those lucky enough to take the 10-minute boat ride to Manhattan stayed put. After all, this great melting pot also was deemed a honey pot, the place to partake of America's prosperity. However, for too many, life wound up being eked out in crowded tenements. The good life would have to wait for second or third generations.

In 1924, stricter federal laws reduced the flood of immigrants to a trickle. It wasn't until 1965, and passage of relaxed policies, that the golden doors reopened. Since then, the flow of

Visitors to the Statue of Liberty loading for the tour boat's next stop, Ellis Island. Left: Museum entrance hall at Ellis Island. The National Park Service welcomes more than two million visitors to these sites each year.

newcomers to Manhattan has outpaced that of any previous eras. They come from India, Malaysia, Vietnam, Syria, the Caribbean, Uruguay – everywhere – providing the cosmopolitan verve that makes New York New York, and one of the few places where you can nosh on wonton, falafel, dosa, jerk pork, and calzone in the same block. What would an erstwhile visitor to New Amsterdam think now, to discover that 180 languages can be heard, and so many cuisines enjoyed, on the city's streets?

Recollection of Celia Adler, immigrant from Russia, arriving at age 12 in 1914

I never saw such a big building – the size of it…. According to the houses I left in my town, this was like a whole city in one…building. It was an enormous thing to see…. I almost felt smaller than I am to see that beautiful [building].

My basket, my little basket – that's all I had with me. There was hardly anything. My mother gave me the sorrah [a sandwich] and I had one change of clothes. That's what I brought from Europe.

Memories of Lazarus Salemon, who arrived from Hungary at age 16 in 1920

I feel like I had two lives. You plant something in the ground. It has roots, and then you transplant it where it stays permanently. That's what happened to me…. I became a man here. All of a sudden, I started life new, amongst people whose language I didn't understand…. Everything was different…but I never despaired. I was optimistic.

And this is the only country where you're not a stranger, because we're all strangers. It's only a matter of time – who got here first.

Both reminiscences from the Ellis Island Oral History Project.

"This is a peaceful countryside and it seems appropriate that we should dedicate this library to the spirit of peace."

Although Franklin Delano Roosevelt spent more time in the White House than any U.S. President, his heart never left the shores of the Hudson River. During World War II, the harried commander in chief often willed himself to sleep via virtual valley reality. He'd close his eyes and imagine a favorite boyhood pastime – sledding down the steep hill behind Springwood, his lifelong home in Hyde Park. Today a national historic site, Springwood still breathes with his indomitable spirit.

FDR's valley roots went deep: the first Roosevelt – Claes Martenszen Van Rosenvelt – immigrated to New Netherland in 1650. That's undoubtedly why Franklin was such an avid student of the region's past. How avid? As New York's governor, he flaunted possible conflict-of-interest laws to continue serving for a spell as Hyde Park's town historian.

Like Thomas Jefferson, Roosevelt had an interest in architecture. His models were not the Roman temples favored by the third president, but the sturdy dwellings familiar to his Dutch forebears. In the 1930s, when it came time to build a series of post offices in and around Hyde Park, he paid the same meticulous attention to their design as he did to the nation's recovery from the Great Depression and gathering war clouds. He insisted they be patterned after local 18th-century homes, using rough fieldstone. The same stones were gathered to

construct his presidential library and museum – the first in the nation – which contains everything from his Oval Office furnishings to his car, specially equipped with hand controls. And he turned again to these simple building blocks when designing his retirement home, Top Cottage, several miles from Springwood. For Roosevelt, this neo-Dutch architecture taught an important civics lesson. "The spirit of simplicity of the homes of our ancestors is a good influence on a civilization which seems to be reverting to the more humble and honest ideals," he said in 1936.

Yet FDR also is responsible for one of the valley's most-visited modern buildings. Throughout World War II, he championed creation of a formal organization, comprised of representatives from all countries, which would secure and maintain peace throughout the world. His vision was realized less than a month after his death in 1945. His legacy lives on in the organization's name, which he coined – the United Nations.

United Nations General Assembly Building. Right: Springwood, the Hyde Park home of Franklin D. Roosevelt.

Franklin D. Roosevelt lays the cornerstone of his presidential library (November 19, 1939)

Half a century ago a small boy took especial delight in climbing an old tree, now unhappily gone, to pick and eat ripe sickle pears. That was about one hundred feet to the west of where I am standing now. And just to the north he used to lie flat between the strawberry rows and eat sun-warmed strawberries—the best in the world. In the spring of the year, in hip rubber boots, he sailed his first toy boats in the surface water formed by the melting snow. In the summer with his dogs he dug into woodchuck holes in this same field, and some of you are standing on top of those holes at this minute. Indeed, the descendants of those same woodchucks still inhabit this field and I hope that, under the auspices of the National Archivist, they will continue to do so for all time.

It has, therefore, been my personal hope that this Library, and the use of it by scholars and visitors, will come to be an integral part of a country scene which the hand of man has not changed very greatly since the days of the Indians who dwelt here three hundred years ago.

We know from simple deduction that these fields were cultivated by the first inhabitants of America—for the oak trees in these fields were striplings three centuries ago, and grew up in open fields as is proved to us by the wide spreading lower branches. Therefore, they grew in open spaces, and the only open spaces in Dutchess County were the cornfields of the Indians.

This is a peaceful countryside and it seems appropriate in this time of strife that we should dedicate this Library to the spirit of peace—peace for the United States and soon, we hope, peace for the world itself.

At the same time we can express the thought that those in the days to come who seek to learn from contemporaneous documents the history of our time will gain a less superficial and more intimate and accurate view of the aspirations and purposes of all kinds of Americans who have been living in these times.

"The United Nations must hold fast to the heritage of freedom won by the struggle of its people."

After serving as America's First Lady, Eleanor Roosevelt became the *world's* First Lady.

When her husband became the nation's 32nd president, Eleanor Roosevelt had no intention of being the traditional White House matron, agonizing over menus for state dinners. Fortunately, FDR also had a more important role in mind for her. Knowing she would never sugarcoat the truth, he appointed her his "eyes and ears," sending her on cross-country trips to report back to him on working conditions and federal relief efforts. Eleanor proved an indefatigable advocate for the downtrodden, especially the nation's still-marginalized African Americans. Though FDR sometimes tired of her constant pleas to provide more aid for the poor and hungry, she never gave up on their behalf.

Memorial rose garden and gravesite of Franklin and Eleanor Roosevelt, Hyde Park. Right: Portrait of the couple at National Park Service visitor center.

Shortly after her husband's death, President Harry Truman named her a delegate to the fledgling United Nations. This was no honorary position: It provided a bigger stage to promote her belief in each individual's basic dignity and worth. Chairing the U.N. Commission on Human Rights – charged with drafting a Universal Declaration of Human Rights – she tirelessly worked her team of legal scholars to craft a simply worded document that would serve as a global constitution, guaranteeing all people "the right to life, liberty and security of person." "I drive hard and when I get home I will be tired! The men on the commission will be also!" she said of her nonstop schedule. One harried committee member jokingly rejoindered that his own rights were violated by Eleanor's frantic pace.

When the declaration was presented to the General Assembly in Paris on December 10, 1948, it was adopted 48-0. Then, in loving tribute, the delegates gave Eleanor Roosevelt a standing ovation.

Val-Kill – the only home Eleanor ever owned, and the only national historic site devoted to a first lady – exemplifies this extraordinary woman's character. It is a simple house, simply furnished, clearly indicative of someone more concerned with grand ideals than grand possessions.

Eleanor Roosevelt's "The Struggle for Human Rights" (September 28, 1948)

It is my belief…that the struggle for democracy and freedom is a critical struggle, for their preservation is essential to the great objective of the United Nations to maintain international peace and security.

Among free men the end cannot justify the means. We know the patterns of totalitarianism—the single political party, the control of schools, press, radio, the arts, the sciences, and the church to support autocratic authority; these are the age-old patterns against which men have struggled for three thousand years. These are the signs of reaction, retreat, and retrogression.

The United Nations must hold fast to the heritage of freedom won by the struggle of its peoples; it must help us to pass it on to generations to come.

The development of the ideal of freedom and its translation into the everyday life of the people in the great areas of the earth is the product of the efforts of many peoples. It is the fruit of a long tradition of vigorous thinking and courageous action. No one race and no one people can claim to have done all the work to achieve greater dignity for human beings and greater freedom to develop human personality. In each generation and in each country there must be a continuation of the struggle and new steps forward must be taken since this is preeminently a field in which to stand still is to retreat….

The future must see the broadening of human rights throughout the world. People who have glimpsed freedom will never be content until they have secured it for themselves. In a true sense, human rights are a fundamental object of law and government in a just society. Human rights exist to the degree that they are respected by people in relations with each other and by governments in relations with their citizens….

People who continue to be denied the respect to which they are entitled as human beings will not acquiesce forever in such denial.

The Charter of the United Nations is a guiding beacon along the way to the achievement of human rights and fundamental freedoms throughout the world. The immediate test is not only the extent to which human rights and freedoms have already been achieved, but the direction in which the world is moving. Is there a faithful compliance with the objectives of the Charter if some countries continue to curtail human rights and freedoms instead of to promote the universal respect for an observance of human rights and freedoms as called for by the Charter?

The place to discuss the issue of human rights is in the forum of the United Nations. The United Nations has been set up as the common meeting ground for nations, where we can consider our mutual problems and take advantage of our differences in experience. It is inherent in our firm attachment to democracy and freedom that we stand always ready to use the fundamental democratic procedures of honest discussion and negotiation. It is now as always our hope that despite the wide differences in approach we face in the world today, we can with mutual good faith in the principles of the United Nations Charter, arrive at a common basis of understanding….

"For the first time, the world looked to New York, not Paris, for its creative cues."

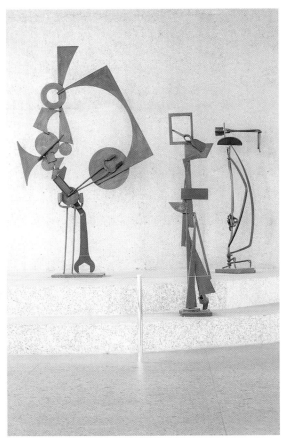

Abstract Expressionist works in Albany's Empire State Plaza Art Collection include sculptures by David Smith and paintings by Jackson Pollock (far left) and Helen Frankenthaler.

Painters of the Hudson River School used the landscape to connect with the public's emotions. In the 1940s, a band of Manhattan artists searched for a fresh way of capturing America's fragile, introspective mood after the nation's costly victory in World War II. To their eyes, representation and geometric abstraction weren't up to the task. So they dared do the unthinkable: paint for the sake of painting, dashing jagged lines and squiggles, drips and blobs, vivid blocks of color – whatever came into their heads at the moment of creation.

At first, the canvases of Jackson Pollock, Robert Motherwell, Mark Rothko, and fellow artists of this New York School shocked the public. Eyes were not accustomed to seeing paintings "about nothing." Soon, however, people caught on. These works explored challenging new ground: the landscape within our souls.

Abstract Expressionism, the popular name for this movement, was the first American art genre to have global influence. For the first time, the world looked to New York, not Paris, for its creative cues.

Two extraordinary valley collections examine the highly personal ways artists followed their muses in the late 20th century. Albany's Empire State Plaza, a modernist office complex, boasts the largest public display of American Abstract Expressionist art, ranging from mammoth outdoor sculptures to mural-sized paintings adorning a quarter-mile-long subterranean corridor. It is one of the greatest legacies of Governor Nelson A. Rockefeller. When overseeing construction of the plaza in the 1960s, he insisted on including funds to purchase art. A decision was made to focus on the New York School, still going strong at the time, so the collection would have immediacy. The works still cast a spell. Visitors often stop dead in their tracks, mesmerized by these 92 colorful, idiosyncratic creations.

Ninety miles downriver, Dia:Beacon thrills on two fronts. The museum is housed in a 1920s Nabisco factory, one of the nation's great examples of adaptive reuse, but hardly, one would think, a fitting place for paintings and sculpture. Yet its airy spaces and generous glass skylights (all original) provide the perfect environment for this collection devoted to 24 masters of the art world's most recent "isms" – conceptualism, minimalism, postmodernism – including Andy Warhol, Sol LeWitt, Richard Serra, and Donald Judd. These boundary-busting creations, most of which would overwhelm a traditional gallery, prove that for artists since the '60s, anything goes. Works here are crafted out of fluorescent lights, string, glass, plywood, even old cars. They may not be your cup of tea, but you'll be talking about them – and the building – for quite some time.

"The principal issue which must be decided is whether the project's effect on the scenic, historical and recreational values of the area are such that we should deny the application."

Pete Seeger and Frances Reese are the valley's environmental icons. One fought for the river with a boat, the *Clearwater*. The other defended a mountain with an institution, Scenic Hudson.

Frances "Franny" Reese looked like your average grandma, but she had the tenacity of your above-average bulldog. In 1963, power company Consolidated Edison proposed building the world's largest pumped-storage hydroelectric plant on Storm King Mountain, forever scarring this Hudson Highlands landmark. Reese joined other outraged citizens in the newly formed Scenic Hudson Preservation Conference. Squaring off against lawyers, government bureaucrats, and corporate executives, they used every trick to block construction of this behemoth that would siphon six billion gallons of river water into a mountaintop reservoir each night, then drop it through electricity-creating turbines during peak-demand daylight hours.

Con Ed's Goliath seemed to have the upper hand over Scenic Hudson's David. The Federal Power Commission granted the utility a license to proceed, in effect decreeing that your average Joe couldn't interfere with the "experts." Armed with a mountain of evidence that the plant would destroy the Highlands' beauty and history, Scenic Hudson took its plight to the U.S. Court of Appeals. On December 29, 1965, it made two historic rulings: 1) common citizens *do* have "standing," the right to sue to protect their environment, and 2) the land's natural and historic importance must be considered when granting such licenses.

Score a bull's-eye for Scenic Hudson. This "Scenic Hudson Decision," as it is popularly called, put natural beauty on an equal legal footing with economics. It ushered in a host of new environmental legislation and organizations. Perhaps most important, it gave citizens nationwide a fighting chance to safeguard their backyards. For all of these reasons, it's considered the birth of the modern grass-roots environmental movement.

Despite this stunning victory, the Storm King battle dragged on until 1980, when Con Ed finally agreed to withdraw its plans. Today, the only power generated on the mountain comes from the legs of hikers climbing to its 1,340-foot summit. Franny Reese saw the struggle through, serving as Scenic Hudson's board chair from 1966 to 1984; she passed away in 2003. Today, the 20,000-member organization – still the valley's chief environmental watchdog – continues following her creed: "Care enough to take some action, do your research so you don't have to backtrack from a position, and don't give up!"

Pete Seeger is a world-famous folksinger – he wrote standards like "Where Have All the Flowers Gone?" and "If I Had a Hammer" – but in the valley he's also renowned for spearheading construction of the *Clearwater*, a replica Hudson River sloop launched in 1969. The object, he says, was to "build a boat to save a river." Today, this "classroom of the waves" carries cargoes of schoolchildren and adults, nearly 13,000 each year, who hoist the sails, sing, and perform scientific experiments while learning about threats to the Hudson and how they can help prevent them. In addition to their ship, the organization Hudson River Sloop Clearwater hosts a popular music festival each June (see page 94) and plays an important advocacy role in protecting the river.

A big win – the Scenic Hudson Decision (1965), giving citizens the right to sue when their environment is threatened

Respondent argues that "petitioners do not have standing to obtain review" because they "make no claim of any personal economic injury resulting from the Commission's action."

Section 313(b) of the Federal Power Act, 16 U.S.C. 825(b), reads:

"(b) Any party to a proceeding under this chapter aggrieved by an order issued by the Commission in such proceeding may obtain a review of such order in the United States Court of Appeals for any circuit wherein the license or public utility to which the order relates is located."

The Commission takes a narrow view of the meaning of "aggrieved party" under the Act. The Supreme Court has observed that the law of standing is a "complicated specialty of federal jurisdiction, the solution of whose problems is in any event more or less determined by the specific circumstances of individual situations"…

The Federal Power Act seeks to protect non-economic as well as economic interests. Indeed, the Commission recognized this in framing the issue in this very case:

"The project is to be physically located in a general area of our nation steeped in the history of the American Revolution and of the colonial period. It is also a general area of great scenic beauty. The principal issue which must be decided is whether the project's effect on the scenic, historical and recreational values of the area are such that we should deny the application."

In order to insure that the Federal Power Commission will adequately protect the public interests in the aesthetic, conservational, and recreational aspects of power development, those who by their activities and conduct have exhibited a special interest in such areas, must be held to be included in the class of "aggrieved" parties… We hold that the Federal Power Act gives petitioners a legal right to protect their special interests…

At an earlier point in these proceedings, the Commission apparently accepted this view. Consolidated Edison strongly objected to the petitioners' standing, but the Commission did not deny their right to file an application for a rehearing under 313(a) of the Act which also speaks in terms of "aggrieved parties."

Moreover, petitioners have sufficient economic interest to establish their standing. The New York-New Jersey Trail Conference, one of the two conservation groups that organized Scenic Hudson, has some seventeen miles of trailways in the area of Storm King Mountain. Portions of these trails would be inundated by the construction of the project's reservoir…

In this case, as in many others, the Commission has claimed to be the representative of the public interest. This role does not permit it to act as an umpire blandly calling balls and strikes for adversaries appearing before it; the right of the public must receive acting and affirmative protection at the hands of the Commission.

The shadow of Storm King Mountain – and its impact on American environmental law – loom over the Hudson.

A Clearwater refrain:
From Pete Seeger's
***"Sailing Down My Dirty Stream"* (1961)**

Sailing down my dirty stream;

Still I love it and I'll keep the dream

That some day though maybe not this year,

My Hudson River will once again run clear.

"The Hudson continues to be very much a working river."

The mantra from the movie *Field of Dreams* applies to New York City: "If you build it, they will come." In fact, the city is undergoing the biggest boom in its history. Construction spending in 2006 reached $21 billion – a record – and all indications are that the figure will soon be surpassed.

Where do the materials come from that fuel Manhattan's skyward thrust? As in the past, often from the Hudson Valley – the same place that supplies water for the city's eight million thirsty residents.

In the early 20th century, valley bricks continued to be Manhattan's chief building blocks. Beacon's Denning's Point Brick Works alone churned out 400,000 each day. Masons stacked millions of them to create landmarks like the Empire State Building and Rockefeller Center. Eventually, cheaper production methods in the Southeast put local brick makers out of business. Powell and Minnock Brick Company in Coeymans closed in 2001, capping a 350-year-old industry along the Hudson.

Still, this continues to be very much a working river: 300 deep-water ships and more than 1,000 tug-towed barges ply its waters each year. Some bring Canadian gypsum to waterfront factories producing wallboard. Others carry cement from inland plants to New York, where it's off-loaded for pouring foundations. Up to a dozen barges tethered together carry crushed stone downstream from valley quarries. At the largest, Tilcon's 1,200-acre Clinton Point quarry, 100-ton trucks haul stone out of a pit reaching 175 feet below the Hudson's surface. There's enough rock left there to last another century.

Gravel-laden barges carrying the harvest of riverside quarries head downriver, furnishing a vital ingredient for Manhattan's concrete foundations. Left: A bulk cargo ship plies the river's 30-foot-deep channel, passing a West Point garden.

Manhattan's 19th-century church spires have been left in the shade by soaring 20th-century "cathedrals of commerce," which in turn are being eclipsed by even taller 21st-century glass and steel towers. This heavenward surge is the city's chief tourist attraction – and the perfect manifestation of the state's motto: "Excelsior," ever upward.

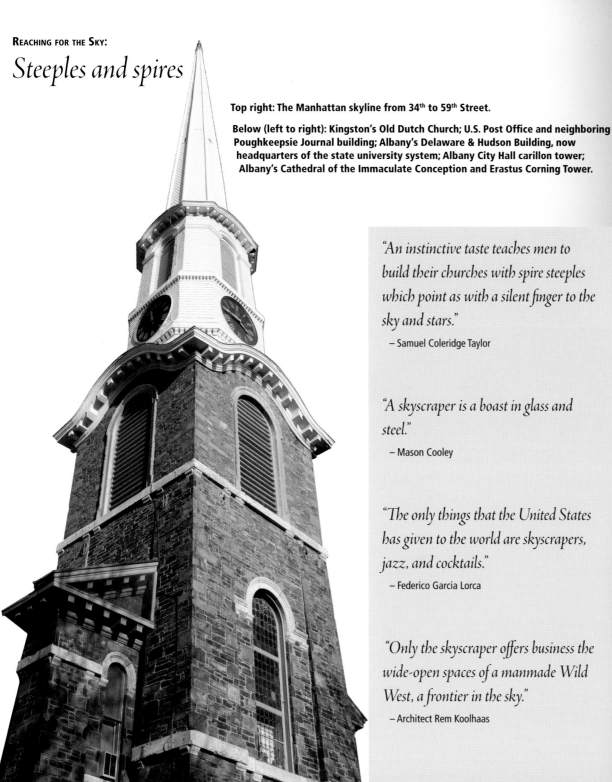

REACHING FOR THE SKY:
Steeples and spires

Top right: The Manhattan skyline from 34th to 59th Street.

Below (left to right): Kingston's Old Dutch Church; U.S. Post Office and neighboring Poughkeepsie Journal building; Albany's Delaware & Hudson Building, now headquarters of the state university system; Albany City Hall carillon tower; Albany's Cathedral of the Immaculate Conception and Erastus Corning Tower.

"An instinctive taste teaches men to build their churches with spire steeples which point as with a silent finger to the sky and stars."

– Samuel Coleridge Taylor

"A skyscraper is a boast in glass and steel."

– Mason Cooley

"The only things that the United States has given to the world are skyscrapers, jazz, and cocktails."

– Federico Garcia Lorca

"Only the skyscraper offers business the wide-open spaces of a manmade Wild West, a frontier in the sky."

– Architect Rem Koolhaas

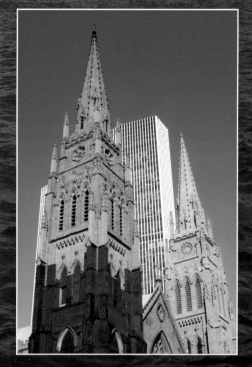

"[The skyscraper] is to the nation what the white church spire is to the village – the visible symbol of aspiration and faith, the white plume saying that the way is up."
– E.B. White

"A chair is a very difficult object. A skyscraper is almost easier. That is why Chippendale is famous."
– Architect Ludwig Mies van der Rohe

"We are defined as Americans by our beliefs – our belief in democracy, the rule of law and respect for human life."

From the earliest European settlers on, the Hudson River Valley has looked to creating a future. Yet it has never lost sight of the past. We *remember*.

Our most poignant memorials honor citizens who sacrificed their lives to preserve freedom. Rare is the village square without a weather-beaten stone soldier guarding a roster of comrades who perished at Chancellorsville, Monte Cassino, or Khe Sanh. Most impressive is the Battle Monument soaring above the U.S. Military Academy's Trophy Point. Inscribed at the base of the polished granite shaft – the largest in the Western Hemisphere – are the names of 2,230 Regular Army officers and enlisted men killed during the Civil War.

Lower Manhattan's Ground Zero is a memorial, too – an invisible one. Yet more powerfully than any statue, the gaping chasm echoes with the senseless brutality of 2,752 innocent lives lost in the 9/11 World Trade Center attacks. Amid this scene of unmatched horror rises another monument: the Freedom Tower. When completed at a height of 1,776 feet, this new skyscraper will proclaim America's steadfast refusal to live in fear of terrorism.

At the National Purple Heart Hall of Honor, opened in 2006, the valley celebrates three centuries of heroism. George Washington created the Badge of Military Merit in 1782 to honor "meritorious Action" of common soldiers, something unheard-of in European armies. The first badges – purple, heart-shaped patches – were awarded the next year to three men at New Windsor Cantonment, the Continental Army's last encampment (and today a state historic site). Renamed the Purple Heart, the citation was revived in 1927 to note the bravery of soldiers killed or injured in armed combat. Some of the first medals were presented to World War I veterans on the cantonment site in 1932. So it's fitting that the Hall of Honor, conceived by valley residents, was erected there as well. Its mission is to collect the stories of all 1.7 million Americans who sacrificed so much for their country.

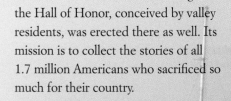

The Hudson Valley remembers (left to right): West Point's Civil War Battle Monument; the 1782 Badge of Military Merit and its 20th-century descendant, the Purple Heart; the World Trade Center.

9/11 – Mayor Rudolph Giuliani's address to the United Nations General Assembly, October 1, 2001

Terrorism is based on the persistent and deliberate violation of fundamental human rights. With bullets and bombs – and now with hijacked airplanes – terrorists deny the dignity of human life. Terrorism preys particularly on cultures and communities that practice openness and tolerance. Their targeting of innocent civilians mocks the efforts of those who seek to live together in peace as neighbors. It defies the very notion of being a neighbor.

This massive attack was intended to break our spirit. It has not done that. It has made us stronger, more determined and more resolved…

The strength of America's response…flows from the principles upon which we stand.

Americans are not a single ethnic group.

Americans are not of one race or one religion.

Americans emerge from all your nations.

We are defined as Americans by our beliefs… Our belief in democracy, the rule of law and respect for human life – that's how you become an American. It is these very principles – and the opportunities these principles give to so many to create a better life for themselves and their families – that make America, and New York, a "shining city on a hill"…

It is tragic and perverse that it is because of these very principles…that we find ourselves under attack by terrorists. Our freedom threatens them because they know that if our ideas of freedom gain a foothold among their people, it will destroy their power. So they strike out against us to keep those ideas from reaching their people.

The best long-term deterrent to terrorism, obviously, is the spread of our principles of freedom, democracy, the rule of law and respect for human life. The more that power spreads around the globe, the safer we will all be. These are very powerful ideas and once they gain a foothold, they cannot be stopped….

Each of you is sitting in this room because of your country's commitment to being part of the family of nations. We need to unite as a family as never before – across all of our differences, in recognition of the fact that the United Nations stands for the proposition that as human beings we have more in common than divides us.

If you need to be reminded of this, you don't need to look very far. Just go outside for a walk in the streets and parks of New York City. You can't walk a block in New York City without seeing somebody that looks different than you, acts different than you, talks different than you, believes different than you….

Freedom from fear is a basic human right. We need to reassert our right to live free from fear with greater confidence and determination than ever before – here in New York City, across America and around the world. With one clear voice, unanimously, we need to say that we will not give in to terrorism.

Surrounded by our friends of every faith, we know that this is not a clash of civilizations; it is a conflict between murderers and humanity.

This is not a question of retaliation or revenge. It is a matter of justice leading to peace. The only acceptable result is the complete and total eradication of terrorism.

New Yorkers are strong and resilient. We are unified. And we will not yield to terror. We do not let fear make our decisions for us.

We choose to live in freedom.

"The Hudson River Valley possesses important historical, cultural, and natural resources."

Boscobel Restoration in Garrison. Left: Picnickers on Boscobel's lawn. Inset: Thomas Rossiter's *Pic-Nic on the Hudson*, 1863; courtesy Julia L. Butterfield Memorial Library, Cold Spring.

The tourist who has a week to spend in the Hudson Valley should get one thing straight: You'll need to come back. The region boasts nearly 100 historic and cultural sites, not to mention awe-inspiring hiking trails, concert halls, wineries, charming towns, antiques shops, lighthouses, five-star restaurants… Gasp!

Many visitors hone in on the intriguing mansions of the privileged class – the Vanderbilts, Rockefellers, and Goulds. The same was true in the 19th century: Travelogues back then gushed over the great houses that lined the Hudson's shores from Yonkers to Albany. The nouveau-riche owners blithely doled out big bucks for the battalions of servants needed to maintain these Gilded Age palaces – even though they graced their marble halls for just a brief spell each summer or fall. Fortunately for us, when these families faded or their fortunes fizzled, many of the finest homes were saved, either by the state or federal government or local organizations. Tours through them today serve as instruction in "how the other half lived," and a primer on the conspicuous consumption of a bygone era.

The Hudson Valley's uniqueness has been recognized in a far-off palace – the U.S. Capitol. In 1996, Congress named the region a National Heritage Area, one of only 37 in the country. Spearheaded by Representative Maurice Hinchey of Saugerties, the designation has provided millions of federal dollars for promoting those sites that explain the valley's singular contribution to American history, culture, and industry. The heritage area complements the work of the Hudson River Valley Greenway, a unique state agency established in 1991 to develop conservation strategies among 242 communities. Its mission is simple yet challenging – to boost economic growth while preserving the historic character and natural beauty of what has been called "the landscape that defined America."

Or in the words of one valley visitor, overwhelmed by its many attractions, "the landscape that defines exhaustion."

In an unusually literate law, Congress designates the Hudson River Valley a National Heritage Area (1996)

Public Law (PL) 104-333

SEC.902. Findings

The Congress finds the following:

1. The Hudson River Valley between Yonkers, New York, and Troy, New York, possesses important historical, cultural, and natural resources, representing themes of settlement and migration, transportation, and commerce.

2. The Hudson River Valley played an important role in the military history of the American Revolution.

3. The Hudson River Valley gave birth to important movements in American art and architecture through the work of Andrew Jackson Downing, Alexander Jackson Davis, Thomas Cole, and their associates, and played a central role in the recognition of the esthetic value of the landscape and the development of the American esthetic ideal.

4. The Hudson River Valley played an important role in the development of the iron, textile, and collar and cuff industries in the 19th century, exemplified in surviving structures such as the Harmony Mills complex at Cohoes, and in the development of early men's and women's labor and cooperative organizations, and is home of the first women's labor union and the first women's secondary school.

5. The Hudson River Valley, in its cities and towns and in its rural landscapes—

A. Displays exceptional surviving physical resources illustrating these themes and the social, industrial, and cultural history of the 19th and early 20th centuries; and

B. Includes many National Historic Sites and Landmarks.

6. The Hudson River Valley is the home of traditions associated with Dutch and Huguenot settlements dating to the 17th and 18th centuries, was the locus of characteristic American stories such as "Rip Van Winkle" and the "Legend of Sleepy Hollow," and retains physical, social, and cultural evidence of these traditions and the traditions of other more recent ethnic and social groups.

7. New York State has established a structure for the Hudson River Valley communities to join together to preserve, conserve, and manage these resources, and to link them through trails and other means, in the Hudson River Greenway Communities Council and the Greenway Conservancy.

SEC. 903. Purpose

The purpose of this title are the following:

1. To recognize the importance of the history and the resources of the Hudson River Valley to the Nation.

2. To assist the State of New York and the communities of the Hudson River Valley in preserving, protecting, and interpreting these resources for the benefit of the Nation.

3. To authorize Federal financial and technical assistance to serve these purposes.

SEC. 904. Hudson River Valley National Heritage Area

Establishment. – There is hereby established a Hudson River Valley National Heritage Area.

1600s—Century of Exploration

1609 (April 4)—Henry Hudson, under contract to the Dutch East India Company, departs from Amsterdam aboard the *Half Moon*.

1609—French explorer Samuel de Champlain is first European to discover lake between present-day New York and Vermont. He names it after himself.

1613 (April 21)—Dutch and Iroquois sign treaty of Taagonshi, agreeing to treat each other "as brothers."

1614—Merchants from the cities of Amsterdam and Hoorn receive a three-year monopoly for fur trading in the Hudson Valley.

1620—Rough seas convince the Pilgrims to settle in Plymouth and not along the Hudson River, their intended destination.

1623—Dutch West India Company established with seven-million guilder investment to settle North America, West Africa, and the Caribbean.

1623—30 families, primarily Walloons (French-speaking refugees from present-day Belgium), arrive aboard the *New Netherland* to settle Fort Orange.

1625 (July 16)—First colonists to settle on Manhattan Island arrive on ship *Eendracht*.

1625—Sarah de Rapaelje is first white child born in New Netherland.

1625—First slaves arrive in the colony.

1638—First school opens in New Amsterdam. Tuition: two beaver pelts a year.

Engravings from *The Hudson, From the Wilderness to the Sea* (1866) by Benson Lossing.

1644—*Short Account of the Mohawk Indians* by Johannes Megapolensis, minister of Rensselaerswyck, is published in Holland. It offers the first in-depth description of Native American life and culture.

1646—Colorful Peter Stuyvesant becomes the fourth and last director general of New Netherland. Known as "old silver nails" for his studded peg leg, he surrenders the colony to England in 1664.

1653—New Amsterdam is chartered as a city. In a first step toward self-government, Peter Stuyvesant appoints "schepens" (aldermen), although he retains right to create ordinances.

OLD DUTCH CHURCH IN ALBANY.

1664—Great Britin seizes New Netherland.

1673—Fleet of 21 Dutch warships retakes colony from Great Britain.

1674—Treaty of Westminster: New Netherland is ceded permanently to Great Britain. New British Governor Edmund Andros decrees English as the colony's official language.

1669—First postal service established between New York City and Albany; mail is carried by Indians.

1683—The Duke of York instructs New York Governor Thomas Dongan to establish a general assembly with the power to enact laws – subject to the approval of Dongan and the duke.

1689—Militia Captain Jacob Leisler stages a coup in New York City, deposing the colony's leaders. He is hanged in 1691.

1694—*Truth Advanced in the Correction of Many Gross & Hurtful Errors* is first book published in New York, by printer William Bradford.

1699—William Kidd, a.k.a. Captain Kidd, is arrested in New York City. The legendary pirate is sent to London, where he is tried and hanged in 1701. His treasure has never been found; some contend it is buried in the Hudson Valley.

1700s—Century of Revolution

1710—3,000 settlers from Palatine region of Germany arrive in New York, settling around Rhinebeck.

1712—Slave plot uncovered to kill New York City's 6,000 inhabitants; 21 are executed in retribution.

1730—Earliest-known painted landscape of the Hudson Valley appears in the background of a portrait of Pau de Wandelaer by Peter Vanderlyn. Work is now in the collection of the Albany Institute of History & Art.

1735—Newspaperman John Peter Zenger is acquitted by a New York jury for "seditious libels" after printing articles critical of Governor William Cosby. The verdict is a milestone in freedom of the press.

1753—Orange County's Jane Colden, America's first female botanist, becomes first scientist to catalogue plants according to the system of Swedish botanist Linnaeus. She publishes New York's first illustrated guide to flora.

1754—Albany Plan – first attempt to unite 13 colonies under a central government – is drafted at meeting of colonial delegates in Albany.

1754—King's College (now Columbia University) founded; state's oldest college and fifth oldest in U.S.

1755-1757—Fort Edward, British stronghold on the Hudson River 50 miles north of Albany, is constructed during the French and Indian War. Encampment for thousands of soldiers, it was the most populous colonial "city" after New York and Boston.

1758—British Army surgeon Richard Shuckburgh composes "Yankee Doodle" at Fort Crailo in present-day Rensselaer. Song pokes fun at colonial troops during French and Indian War.

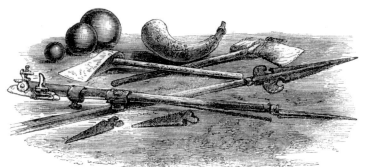

RELICS FROM THE BATTLE-FIELD.

1766—Mehitabel Prendergast rides 80 miles nonstop from Dutchess County to New York City to plead for a pardon for her husband, sentenced to hang for fomenting tenant riots against landowners' high rents. She won a reprieve; her husband was eventually pardoned.

1766—Arent Traphagen opens tavern in the center of Rhinebeck. Later renamed the Beekman Arms, it is America's oldest continuously operating hostelry.

1767—Indian emissary Sir William Johnson is first white man to visit Saratoga Springs and enjoy mineral waters.

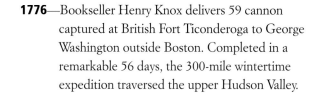

1776—Bookseller Henry Knox delivers 59 cannon captured at British Fort Ticonderoga to George Washington outside Boston. Completed in a remarkable 56 days, the 300-mile wintertime expedition traversed the upper Hudson Valley.

1776 (August 26-29)—The Battle of Brooklyn. Washington's army barely escapes a rout.

1776 (November 15)—Americans defeated at Battle of Fort Washington; they suffer 2,900 casualties, most taken prisoner.

1776—The *Turtle*, world's first submarine, fails in an attempt to blow up a British ship in the Hudson River.

1776 (September 21)—One-quarter of Manhattan is destroyed by fire. Historians still debate whether it was arson or accident.

1776—British begin housing American prisoners in filthy, disease-ridden ships docked in the East River off Brooklyn; between 7,500 and 11,000 soldiers die in them during the course of the war – far more than are killed in battle.

1777 (October 6-13)—British capture Forts Montgomery and Clinton in the Hudson Highlands, breaking through the first river-blocking chain across the Hudson, then burn Kingston, first state capital.

1777 (April 26)—16-year-old Sybil Ludington – the Hudson Valley's Paul Revere – completes a 40-mile "midnight ride" to warn her father's Putnam County militia of a British threat to nearby Danbury, Connecticut.

1777—George Clinton of Little Britain becomes the state's first governor. He is elected six straight times, serving until 1795, and wins a seventh term in 1800. In 1804, he is elected U.S. vice president to Thomas Jefferson.

1783 (November 25)—British evacuate New York City.

1783—Nantucket Quakers relocate to Hudson and establish the city as a bustling whaling port.

1784—*Empress of China* – first American ship in the China trade – is built in Albany.

1785—The *Poughkeepsie Journal* – oldest newspaper in New York State – goes to press.

1792 (May 17)—24 brokers and merchants sign an agreement beneath a buttonwood tree on Wall Street, founding the New York Stock Exchange.

1797—Albany becomes state capital.

1797—Slave Isabella Baumfree is born in Ulster County. She eventually escapes, renames herself Sojourner Truth, and becomes a popular speaker and advocate for abolition and women's rights.

1800s—Century of Innovation

1801—Artist Charles Willson Peale unearths prehistoric mastodon bones on Orange County farms. A reassembled skeleton becomes the prime attraction at his Philadelphia natural history museum.

1804—Hachaliah Bailey of Somers acquires an African elephant to do farm work. "Old Bet" proves such an attraction that he takes her on tour, marking the birth of the American circus.

1812—Artist John Vanderlyn of Kingston paints *Ariadne Asleep on the Isle of Naxos*, the first large-scale nude displayed in the United States. It causes a sensation.

POUGHKEEPSIE, FROM LEWISBURG.

1821—Educator Emma Willard establishes the Troy Female Seminary (today known as the Emma Willard School), first academic institution for young women.

1823—Catskill Mountain House – next to Niagara Falls, America's most popular 19th-century tourist destination – opens atop an escarpment in the Catskill Mountains. The hotel closes in 1942.

1823—"A Visit from St. Nicholas" ("'Twas the night before Christmas…") first appears in the *Troy Sentinel*. Its authorship is commonly attributed to Clement Clark Moore.

1824—James Fenimore Cooper visits a cave in the Hudson River at Glens Falls. It features prominently in his most popular novel, *The Last of the Mohicans*, published in 1826.

1828—The Delaware & Hudson Canal is completed. The country's first $1 million private investment project, the 108-mile waterway connects Pennsylvania coalfields to the Hudson River.

1829—Joseph Henry, a teacher at the Albany Academy, perfects the electromagnet; one magnet of his supports 2,086 pounds, then a world's record. His work contributes to inventions of the telegraph and electric motor.

1836—Martin Van Buren of Kinderhook is elected President. When granting written approval, he uses the initials "O.K.," short for his nickname, "Old Kinderhook."

1839—Shoemaker John Jacques opens a commercial winery in Washingtonville. Now known as Brotherhood Winery, it's the oldest continuously operating vintner in America.

1841—First Dutchess County Fair held. Today, it's the state's second-largest agricultural exhibition.

1842—Croton Aqueduct is completed. An engineering marvel, the 41-mile underground masonry tunnel delivered fresh water to New York City from a reservoir in Westchester County. Today it is a linear state park.

1849—Stallion Hambletonian is foaled on a Sugar Loaf farm. Though not a racer, he had good genes: 99 percent of standardbred horses in North American harness racing today trace their descent to him.

1850—Washington's Headquarters in Newburgh becomes the first publicly operated historic site in the U.S.

1853—Chef at Moon's Lake House in Saratoga Springs invents the potato chip. The snack was created as a rebuke to a customer who complained that the fried potatoes were too "thick and greasy."

1860—Popular hymn "Jesus Loves Me" – written by Anna Warner of Constitution Island (across from West Point) – is published.

1863—New York City draft riots. Laborers protest federal act allowing the rich to elude Civil War service by paying $300. Damages top $1.5 million and casualties reach 1,000 in four-day melee.

1863—Saratoga Racetrack opens; Thoroughbred Lizzie W is first horse to cross the finish line.

1864—Irish immigrant Kate Mullaney organizes the country's first female labor union – the Collar Laundry Union – with 300 fellow workers in Troy.

1865—First students matriculate at Poughkeepsie's Vassar College. Founded by brewer Matthew Vassar, it's the first U.S. college offering women the opportunity to study art history, chemistry, and geology. Professor Maria Mitchell is first recognized woman astronomer.

1870—Metropolitan Museum of Art is founded with 174 paintings purchased from three European collections.

1870—The Equitable Building – America's first skyscraper – opens in Manhattan. Seven stories tall, the tower also boasted the first passenger elevators.

1884—Thomas Edison supervises construction in Newburgh of one of first U.S. electric generating stations. City becomes the second municipality (after New York) to be electrified by the inventor.

1885 (July 23)—Ulysses S. Grant, president and Civil War's winning general, dies in a cottage atop Mount McGregor, near Saratoga Springs. He had just completed his memoirs.

THE PALISADES.

1886 (October 28)—Statue of Liberty – a gift from the people of France – is dedicated. Meant to mark the U.S. centennial in 1876, it is completed 10 years late because of difficulty in funding construction of the base.

1888—With an apple tree for their clubhouse, a handful of duffers in Yonkers found St. Andrew's, America's oldest continuously operating golf club.

1895—The first national crew-racing championship takes place on the Hudson in Poughkeepsie. One of America's top sporting events, the Poughkeepsie Regatta continues until 1949.

1899—Theodore Roosevelt is first governor to take oath of office in Albany's state capitol, which he declares "completed." Unfinished Romanesque-French Renaissance building had been under construction for 32 years and cost $25 million.

1900s—Century of Preservation

1900—Yaddo, the Saratoga Springs estate of financier Spencer Trask, becomes one of America's premier arts colonies. Residents have included composer Aaron Copland, writers Sylvia Plath and Truman Capote, and artist Milton Avery.

1901 (September 13)—Hiking up the Adirondacks' Mt. Marcy, Vice President Theodore Roosevelt is alerted by messenger that President William McKinley, shot by an assassin in Buffalo six days earlier, is worsening. A perilous 35-mile nighttime stage ride delivers him to a train in North Creek for the trip to the dying McKinley's bedside.

1902—Mount Beacon Incline Railway opens, carrying sightseers to top of 1,500-foot slope. The cable railway, designed by Otis Elevator Corp., was the world's steepest.

1903—Byrdcliffe, utopian arts and crafts community near Woodstock, opens. Today, furniture, metalwork, and pottery made there is highly prized.

1907—Ball begins its maiden descent from the flagpole atop Manhattan's One Times Square to mark the New Year.

1910—Pilot Glenn Curtiss flies 137 miles from Albany to Manhattan, capturing the U.S. distance record. He also delivers the first airmail letter, from mayor of Albany to mayor of New York.

1915—West Point's "The class the stars fell on." A third of the year's 164 graduates became generals. Dwight Eisenhower and Omar Bradley each earn five stars.

1919—Madam C.J. Walker – recognized as America's first female self-made millionaire – dies at Villa Lewaro, her Irvington mansion. The former Mississippi cotton picker founded a company that manufactured popular hair-straightening products.

1921—Nature writer John Burroughs dies. Theodore Roosevelt, Henry Ford, and Thomas Edison were among those who visited him at Slabsides, the rustic retreat he built in Ulster County.

1922—First issue of *Reader's Digest* is published by DeWitt and Lila Acheson Wallace from a basement office beneath a Greenwich Village speakeasy.

1923—First game played in Yankee Stadium. New York Yankees win 4-1 over rival Boston Red Sox on Babe Ruth's three-run home run.

1923—First section of Appalachian Trail, eventually stretching 2,160 miles from Georgia to Maine, is completed in Bear Mountain State Park.

1924—First cars cross Bear Mountain Bridge. Its 1,632-foot span made it the world's longest suspension bridge.

1928—Playland, America's first planned amusement park, opens in Rye. Seven original rides still thrill visitors to the Art Deco gem listed on the National Register of Historic Places.

1939—Britain's King George VI and his wife, Queen Elizabeth, visit President Franklin D. Roosevelt at his Hyde Park home. The president serves the royal couple hot dogs and makes them cocktails.

1943—Piermont Pier on the Tappan Zee becomes a chief embarkation point for G.I.s headed to World War II battlefields in Europe, earning it the nickname "Last Stop U.S.A."

1944—Bobbysoxers riot over Frank Sinatra's performances at the Paramount Theatre in Manhattan.

1948—Jackson Pollock exhibits the first of his "drip paintings" – created by pouring and swirling paint over canvases laid on his studio floor – at Manhattan's Betty Parsons Gallery. A year later, he is hailed as "the greatest living American artist."

1949—Cornerstone is laid for United Nations building in Manhattan. The 18-acre site was acquired two years earlier with an $8.5 million gift from John D. Rockefeller Jr.

1953—Convicted spies Julius and Ethel Rosenberg are executed in the electric chair at Sing Sing Prison in Ossining.

1958—Nelson Aldrich Rockefeller of Pocantico Hills is elected to the first of four consecutive terms as governor. Grandson of John D. Rockefeller, he vastly expanded the state's parks, highway, and university systems. He was appointed U.S. vice president by Gerald Ford.

1959—Spiraling Guggenheim Museum opens in Manhattan. One critic contends that "it is less a museum than a monument" to its architect, Frank Lloyd Wright, who'd died six months earlier.

1966—The Hudson River Fisherman's Association is founded. Later renamed Riverkeeper, the organization has identified hundreds of polluters, who have been forced to pay millions of dollars in fines. The money is used to clean up the Hudson.

1972—The Culinary Institute of America – the nation's leading cooking school and one of the Hudson Valley's prime tourist attractions – relocates from Connecticut to a former Jesuit monastery in Hyde Park.

1981—Hudson River Foundation, the valley's leading scientific research organization, is established with $12 million in funds contributed by power plants to settle the Con Edison Storm King case.

1984—Albany native William Kennedy wins the Pulitzer Prize for *Ironweed*. Set in the capital, the novel is part of the author's "Albany trilogy."

1998—President Clinton names the Hudson one of 14 American Heritage Rivers. The designation provides federal support to protect and preserve the waterway's natural beauty and cultural heritage.

2002—IBM opens the world's most technologically advanced 300 mm chip-making plant in East Fishkill. The $2.5 billion project is the largest private-sector investment in New York State history.

An Invitation from Reed Sparling

Mid-September in the Hudson Valley: Summer heat is giving way grudgingly to fall crispness, an inducement for leaves to begin their spectacular transformation. Branches bowed down with apples await relief from eager pickers, up from the city for a dose of fresh air and the ingredients for a homemade pie. Pillowy clouds keep pace with sailboats surging through the river's chop, both beneficiaries of a steady breeze.

It's a perfect day for a ramble—a Hudson River Valley Ramble. Each September, the Hudson River Valley National Heritage Area (*www. hudsonrivervalley.com*), in conjunction with the Hudson River Valley Greenway and other organizations, hosts a two-weekend-long series of guided walks, hikes, pedals, and paddles highlighting the region's historic and natural treasures. Ranging in location from a Rensselaer County mountaintop to the canyons of lower Manhattan, these activities attract all ages and skill sets. Boots muddied from scaling the Catskills' high peaks stride next to sneakers right out of the box.

Their wearers are in for a treat and a story. Actually, two stories – both about time. On the one hand, the Ramble celebrates time's passage. These treks follow paths trod by nameless Native Americans and destiny-defining Presidents. They cross fields stained by Patriot blood or exploited to fuel an industrial revolution. The walks also illustrate how fervently we treasure our past by striving to protect these special places.

Obviously, the valley is not the wilderness that captivated Henry Hudson in 1609; he didn't sail past the minaret-like towers of the Indian Point nuclear power plant. Like the tides that reverse the river's current twice a day, its natural fortunes ebb and flow. Less than 50 years ago, the Hudson was an open sewer, a convenient dumping ground for industrial toxins and community waste. The only people who swam in it did so out of necessity – because they'd fallen in. Those who wanted to paddle its quiet coves had to search long and hard for access points. Its wildlife dwindling, the river appeared down for the count.

Today, the tide has turned in the Hudson's favor:

- Moms sunbathing on the sand at Kingston Point Beach watch their children's horseplay in the river. After a container ship passes, the youngsters grab their boogie boards, gleefully anticipating the mammoth vessel's approaching wake, which will propel them shoreward.

Richard B. Fisher Center for the Performing Arts at Bard College.

- Beneath the ship, Atlantic sturgeon – the Hudson's largest creatures, weighing up to 800 pounds and spanning seven feet – scour the river bottom for food. Older than the dinosaurs, these spiny fish once were caught in such abundance that their delectable flesh was dubbed "Albany beef." Over-fished nearly to extinction in the Hudson, successful efforts are now underway to reintroduce them to the river.

- A kayaker enjoying the solitude of Catskills' RamsHorn-Livingston Sanctuary trades glances with a bald eagle, perched high overhead. Their local nesting grounds decimated by rapacious development, the birds had become itinerants, appearing in the valley only during winters when food was scarce in their frozen Canadian habitat. Today, the majestic raptors are again year-round residents, and their population is growing. How miraculous is this? Check out the figures: Sixty hatched here in the last eight years, none in the previous 100.

What's behind this comeback? People who care. Fortunately, they appear in every generation, often when it seems things couldn't get any worse. Some are professionals, like the experts at Scenic Hudson, Riverkeeper, the Open Space Institute, or the state's Hudson River Estuary Program. But far more are common citizens willing to add another commitment to their busy lives. Why do they do it? Because for many, the Hudson River Valley is more than a place; it's a way of life. And when their life – or an integral part of it – is threatened, they make a racket.

The City of Hudson was a major 19th-century whaling port; in the 20th century, it fell on hard times. For the last decade it's been enjoying a renaissance as one of the region's premier antiquing destinations. On weekends, its main street buzzes with tourists hunting for bargains and a table in one of its myriad upscale restaurants.

So imagine the dismay when the St. Lawrence Cement Company announced plans in 1999 to build a $353 million coal-fired cement plant there. Destined to be the largest facility of its kind in the nation, it would feature a 400-foot smokestack and numerous other skyscraper-size buildings, all viewable from some of the region's most iconic historic and natural sites. It was the biggest threat to the Hudson Valley since 1963, when utility Consolidated Edison decided to construct a hydroelectric plant on Storm King Mountain, a Hudson Highlands landmark. And like that earlier monstrosity, it aroused citizens' outrage.

As in the fight to stymie Con Ed, those battling St. Lawrence resorted to a host of tactics – holding bake sales to pay lawyers' fees, spreading the word about the plant's potential pollution and noise, rallying residents to speak out at public meetings, instigating letter-writing campaigns, putting "STOP THE PLANT" signs on lawns and in shop windows.

It took 17 years for Con Ed to back down; St. Lawrence pulled out after six – the day after New York's Department of State ruled that a facility of such magnitude had no place in a region whose economy depends on tourism and recreation. Once again, the people prevailed.

Clearwater Pumpkin Festival on the Beacon waterfront.

The wild columbine is an early spring bloomer at forest edge and meadow boundary.

If the Hudson River Valley is a way of life, it takes a lifetime to get to know it. Just when you think you've "seen it all," along comes a new discovery. Hiking in the Catskills is always an invigorating experience, physically and spiritually. God has created marvels here. On Twin Mountain, however, man's handiwork momentarily amazes. Turning a sharp corner, one crosses a field of rubble, leftovers from an old quarry. In its midst stand several huge thrones, crafted out of the ubiquitous flat rocks, each facing a delicious panoramic view. Sitting in this mini Machu Picchu, you feel like king of the world.

Or how about this: You've toured all the valley's historic houses. I'll wager you haven't been to Stepping Stones (*www.steppingstones. org*). Miniscule by Vanderbilt standards – and furnished with an eye toward comfort, not show – this Westchester County Colonial packs a bigger emotional punch. That's because *Time* magazine deemed its owner one of the 100 most-influential people of the 20th century, on equal footing with Albert Einstein and Gandhi. It was the residence of Bill Wilson, founder of Alcoholics Anonymous. There in the kitchen sits the battered table on which he drew up the 12-step program that's saved millions of lives.

Again, it's determined people who make these surprises possible. Fort Montgomery played a pivotal role in the American Revolution; the British attacked it in 1777, during the Saratoga Campaign. A decade ago, you had to crawl beneath tangled vines and blown-down trees to inspect its redoubts, among the most intact from the war.

It was so hidden that then-Governor George Pataki, an admitted history buff who lives nearby, wasn't aware of the fort's existence. Today, thanks to a cadre of citizens who convinced the state to preserve the site, you can follow pathways past foundations of its barracks and those redoubts where Redcoats overran local militiamen.

Variety being the spice of life, the Hudson Valley rates as a five-alarm chili. Some regions of the country may rival it architecturally. Others boast an equally vivid history or similarly dramatic landscapes. You can find great concert halls and restaurants in lots of places. But nowhere outside the valley will you discover all of these – and so much more – in such mind-boggling profusion.

Check out this sample itinerary. Enjoy breakfast at the Saratoga Racetrack (*www.saratogaracetrack.com*), just feet from thundering Thoroughbreds undergoing a morning workout. Enjoy your own workout by strolling around Saratoga Battlefield, where the tide of the American Revolution began to change. After devouring a sandwich stuffed with local produce and cheese (on homemade bread, naturally), soak in a spectacular collection of Abstract Expressionist art in Albany. Then drive down the Taconic State Parkway, through rolling farm fields with thrilling views of the distant Catskills. You've barely got time for dinner, served up by a master chef trained at Hyde Park's world-renowned Culinary Institute of America (*www.ciachef.edu*). Your day ends with some first-class theater – and a gorgeous Hudson Highlands sunset – via the Hudson Valley Shakespeare Festival at Boscobel, one of the region's grandest estates.

Thank goodness you're booked for the night in a nearby bed and breakfast. Tomorrow's schedule includes a winery tour, a couple of historic houses, a hike, and a concert at Poughkeepsie's Bardavon 1869 Opera House, where Mark Twain and John Philip Sousa once thrilled audiences.

If this pace is too hectic, simply sample a few of the valley's villages and cities. Some are architectural time capsules. For example, strolling down Hurley's main street, lined with 18th-century Dutch homes, you'll almost feel out of place without a tri-cornered hat. In Athens, you can marvel at how the output of local brickworks was turned into such elegant, Federal-period houses.

For years, people steered clear of the valley's decaying urban centers, emptied out in the '60s and '70s in favor of the suburban shopping mall. Even locals wouldn't

Garrison Resort in the Hudson Highlands. Right: When opened in 1924, the Bear Mountain Bridge was the world's longest suspension span.

head downtown unless they had a pressing reason, like renewing a driver's license. Today, however, its cities are on the upswing. From Yonkers to Albany, Peekskill to Kingston, new life is being breathed into old buildings, often by artists in need of large spaces to work. Their pioneering spirit lures others to open restaurants, shops, and galleries.

One weekend a month, many valley burgs celebrate their newfound success with citywide celebrations – gallery openings, concerts, poetry readings, farmers' markets. At a recent Second Saturday in Beacon, once-derelict sidewalks were teeming. More forcefully then words, the bustle announced loud and clear, "This place is going to make it."

Unbridled optimism. Those 17th-century Dutch settlers who dared to tame the valley's wilderness had it. So do many of the region's 21st-century residents. How else can you explain the Greenway's audacious goal of creating two 150-mile-long linear parks along both shores of the Hudson? Or the moxie of citizens who formed an organization to purchase the Poughkeepsie Railroad Bridge?

Anywhere else, the 6,767-foot span – the world's longest when opened in 1888 – would have been demolished. After all, the last train crossed it three decades ago. But as this book attests, the Hudson Valley is a spawning ground for dreamers. And that's why, if all goes according to plan, when the replica *Half Moon* reaches Poughkeepsie during its 2009 sail commemorating the 400th anniversary of Henry Hudson's upriver voyage, crowds will be cheering from atop the magnificent Walkway Over the Hudson (*www.walkway.org*), a 212-foot-high aerie from which to survey the region's splendor.

Now, that's something to celebrate in its own right – and a surefire destination for future Hudson River Valley Rambles.

Hudson Valley Map

Hudson River Watershed

© 2007 Involvement Media, Inc.

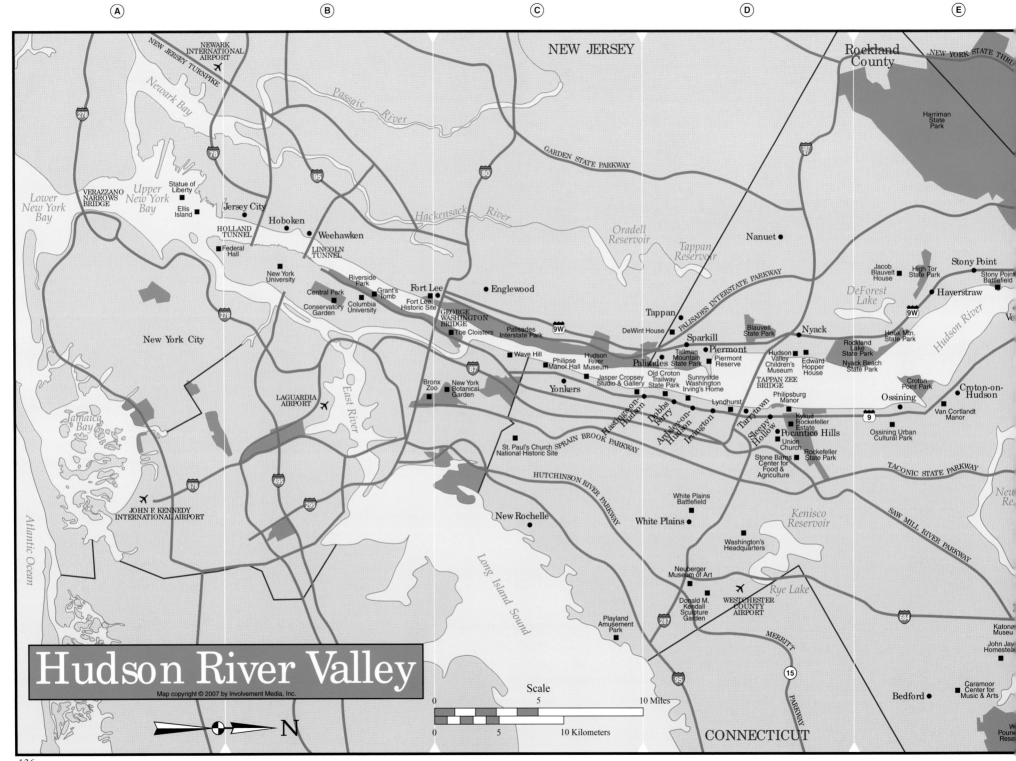

Hudson River Valley

Map copyright © 2007 by Involvement Media, Inc.

Scale

0 .... 5 .... 10 Miles

0 .... 5 .... 10 Kilometers

N

A   **B**   **C**   **D**   **E**

NEW JERSEY

Rockland County

NEW YORK STATE THRU

NEWARK INTERNATIONAL AIRPORT

New Jersey Turnpike

Passaic River

Harriman State Park

278

78

95

Newark Bay

GARDEN STATE PARKWAY

80

287

Lower New York Bay

Upper New York Bay

Statue of Liberty

Ellis Island

Jersey City

Hoboken

Weehawken

Hackensack River

Oradell Reservoir

Tappan Reservoir

Nanuet

Jacob Blauvelt House

High Tor State Park

Stony Point

Stony Point Battlefield

VERAZZANO NARROWS BRIDGE

HOLLAND TUNNEL

Federal Hall

LINCOLN TUNNEL

New York University

Riverside Park

Grant's Tomb

Fort Lee

Englewood

DeForest Lake

9W

Haverstraw

Hudson River

Central Park

Conservatory Garden

Columbia University

Fort Lee Historic Site

GEORGE WASHINGTON BRIDGE

Tappan

DeWint House

PALISADES INTERSTATE PARKWAY

Blauvelt State Park

Nyack

Hook Mtn. State Park

278

The Cloisters

Palisades Interstate Park

9W

Sparkill

Tallman Mountain State Park

Piermont

Piermont Reserve

Hudson Valley Children's Museum

Edward Hopper House

Rockland Lake State Park

Nyack Beach State Park

New York City

Wave Hill

Philipse Manor Hall

Hudson River Museum

Palisades

87

Jasper Cropsey Studio & Gallery

Old Croton Trailway State Park

Sunnyside Washington Irving's Home

Hudson Estate

TAPPAN ZEE BRIDGE

Croton Point Park

Ossining

Croton-on-Hudson

Bronx Zoo

New York Botanical Garden

Yonkers

Hastings-on-Hudson

Dobbs Ferry

Ardsley-on-Hudson

Irvington

Lyndhurst

Tarrytown

Sleepy Hollow

Philipsburg Manor

Kykuit Rockefeller Estate

Van Cortlandt Manor

9

Ossining Urban Cultural Park

LAGUARDIA AIRPORT

East River

Jamaica Bay

Pocantico Hills

Union Church

Rockefeller State Park

St. Paul's Church National Historic Site

SPRAIN BROOK PARKWAY

Stone Barns Center for Food & Agriculture

TACONIC STATE PARKWAY

678

495

295

HUTCHINSON RIVER PARKWAY

JOHN F. KENNEDY INTERNATIONAL AIRPORT

White Plains Battlefield

Kenisco Reservoir

SAW MILL RIVER PARKWAY

Atlantic Ocean

New Rochelle

White Plains

Washington's Headquarters

684

Long Island Sound

Neuberger Museum of Art

Rye Lake

Katonah Museum

John Jay Homestead

Playland Amusement Park

Donald M. Kendall Sculpture Garden

287

WESTCHESTER COUNTY AIRPORT

95

MERRITT

15

PARKWAY

Caramoor Center for Music & Arts

Bedford

CONNECTICUT

138

Hudson Valley Voyage

Historic, Cultural, and Recreational Treasures
from New York City to Poughkeepsie

Tourism information for all of
the National Heritage Area sites
on this map can be found on
pages 140 to 143.

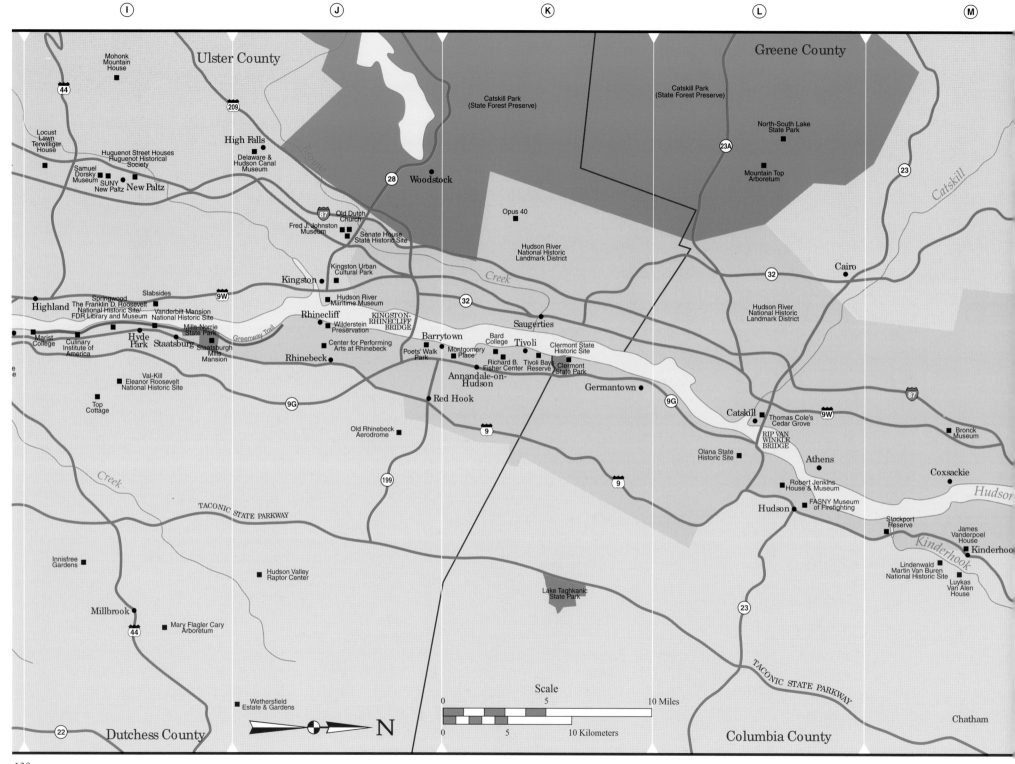

Ulster County

Greene County

Mohonk
Mountain
House

44

209

Locust
Lawn
Terwilliger
House

Huguenot Street Houses
Huguenot Historical
Society

Samuel
Dorsky
Museum
SUNY
New Paltz
New Paltz

High Falls

Delaware &
Hudson Canal
Museum

Catskill Park
(State Forest Preserve)

Catskill Park
(State Forest Preserve)

North-South Lake
State Park

23A

Mountain Top
Arboretum

23

28
Woodstock

Old Dutch
Church
Fred J. Johnston
Museum
Senate House
State Historic Site

87

Opus 40

Hudson River
National Historic
Landmark District

32

Cairo

Kingston Urban
Cultural Park

Kingston

Creek

Springwood
Slabsides
The Franklin D. Roosevelt
National Historic Site/
FDR Library and Museum

Highland

9W

Hudson River
Maritime Museum

Vanderbilt Mansion
National Historic Site

Marist
College
Culinary
Institute of
America

Hyde
Park
Staatsburg

Mills-Norrie
State Park

Greenway Trail

Rhinecliff

Wilderstein
Preservation

Saugerties

KINGSTON-
RHINECLIFF
BRIDGE

Hudson River
National Historic
Landmark District

Center for Performing
Arts at Rhinebeck

Rhinebeck

Staatsburgh
Mills
Mansion

Barrytown

Bard
College
Tivoli

Poets' Walk
Park

Montgomery
Place

Richard B.
Fisher Center
Tivoli Bays
Reserve

Clermont State
Historic Site

Clermont
State Park

Catskill

Thomas Cole's
Cedar Grove

9W

87

Val-Kill
Eleanor Roosevelt
National Historic Site

9G

Annandale-on-
Hudson

Germantown

9G

RIP VAN
WINKLE
BRIDGE

Bronck
Museum

Top
Cottage

Red Hook

Athens

Coxsackie

Old Rhinebeck
Aerodrome

9

Olana State
Historic Site

199

9

Hudson

FASNY Museum
of Firefighting

Robert Jenkins
House & Museum

Hudson

Creek

TACONIC STATE PARKWAY

Stockport
Reserve

Kinderhook

James
Vanderpoel
House
Kinderhook

Innisfree
Gardens

Hudson Valley
Raptor Center

Lindenwald
Martin Van Buren
National Historic Site
Luykas
Van Alen
House

Lake Taghkanic
State Park

Millbrook

44
Mary Flagler Cary
Arboretum

23

TACONIC STATE PARKWAY

Wethersfield
Estate & Gardens

N

22

Dutchess County

Columbia County

Chatham

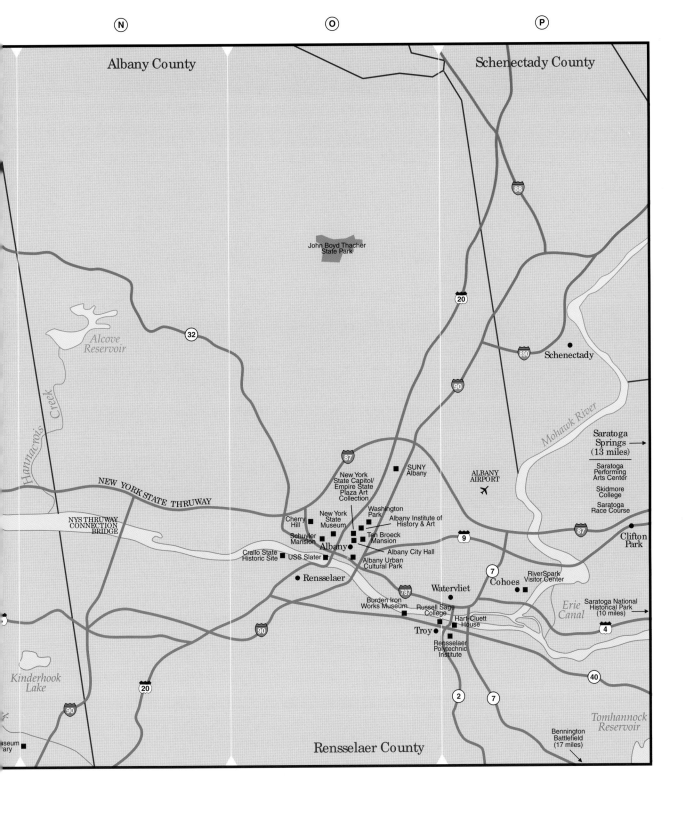

Albany County   Schenectady County

John Boyd Thacher
State Park

Alcove
Reservoir

Hannacrois Creek

32

88

20

890

Schenectady

90

Mohawk River

87

NEW YORK STATE THRUWAY

NYS THRUWAY
CONNECTION
BRIDGE

SUNY
Albany

New York
State Capitol/
Empire State
Plaza Art
Collection

ALBANY
AIRPORT

Washington
Park

Cherry
Hill

New York
State
Museum

Albany Institute of
History & Art

Schuyler
Mansion

Ten Broeck
Mansion

Crailo State
Historic Site

Albany

USS Slater

Albany City Hall

9

87

Clifton
Park

Saratoga
Springs
(13 miles)

Saratoga
Performing
Arts Center

Skidmore
College

Saratoga
Race Course

Hudson Valley Voyage

*Historic, Cultural, and Recreational Treasures
from Hyde Park to Saratoga*

**Tourism information for all of
the National Heritage Area sites
on this map can be found on
pages 140 to 143.**

Albany Urban
Cultural Park

Rensselaer

7

Cohoes

RiverSpark
Visitor Center

787

Watervliet

Burden Iron
Works Museum

Russell Sage
College

Hart-Cluett
House

Erie
Canal

Saratoga National
Historical Park
(10 miles)

90

20

Kinderhook
Lake

Troy

Rensselaer
Polytechnic
Institute

2

7

40

4

Bennington
Battlefield
(17 miles)

Tomhannock
Reservoir

useum
ary

Rensselaer County

Hudson River Valley Heritage Area Sites – *A Guide to the Region's Historic, Cultural, and Recreational Treasures*

Letters in parentheses refer to location letters at top of map.

Albany City Hall (O)
24 Eagle St.
Albany, NY 12210
518-434-5100
Romanesque-style landmark designed by noted 19th-century architect H.H. Richardson.

Albany Institute of History & Art (O)
125 Washington Ave.
Albany, NY 12210
518-463-4478
www.albanyinstitute.org
Fine collections of Hudson River School paintings, portraits of early Dutch settlers.

Bear Mountain State Park (F)
Rte. 9W
Bear Mountain, NY 10911
845-786-2701, ext. 263
www.nysparks.state.ny.us/parks
Adirondacks-style inn; pool, museums, zoo, merry-go-round.

**Bennington Battlefield
State Historic Site** (P)
Rte. 67
Walloomsac, NY 12090
518-686-7109
www.nysparks.state.ny.us/parks
Site of 1777 skirmish between Contintental militia and Hessian mercenaries.

Boscobel (F)
1601 Rte. 9D
Garrison, NY 10524
845-265-3638
www.boscobel.org
One of America's finest Federal-period homes; gardens, nature trail.

Bronck Museum (M)
Rte. 9W
Coxsackie, NY 12051
518-731-6490
www.gchistory.org
Hudson Valley's oldest house, earliest section built 1663; unique 13-sided barn.

Burden Iron Works Museum (O)
1 E. Industrial Parkway
Troy, NY 12180
518-274-5267
www.hudsonmohawkgateway.org
Explores city's industrial history.

Caramoor (E)
149 Girdle Ridge Rd.
Katonah, NY 10536
914-232-5035
www.caramoor.org
Period rooms from Renaissance Europe adorn Mediterranean-style villa; gardens.

Cherry Hill (O)
523½ South Pearl St.
Albany, NY 12202
518-434-4791
www.historiccherryhill.org
Georgian-style residence of prominent Van Rensselaer family.

Clermont State Historic Site (K)
1 Clermont Ave.
Germantown, NY 12526
518-537-4240
www.friendsofclermont.org
Home of Robert Livingston, drafter of Declaration of Independence, negotiator of Louisiana Purchase.

Clove Furnace (E)
21 Clove Furnace Dr.
Arden, NY 10910
845-351-4696
Important 19th-century iron-making site.

Constitution Island (F)
West Point, NY 10996
845-446-8676
www.constitutionisland.org
Revolutionary War fortifications; home of best-selling 19th-century authors Susan and Anna Warner.

Crailo State Historic Site (O)
9½ Riverside Ave.
Rensselaer, NY 12144
518-463-8738
www.nysparks.state.ny.us/parks
Museum of Hudson Valley Dutch settlement.

Delaware & Hudson Canal Museum (J)
23 Mohonk Rd.
High Falls, NY
845-687-9311
www.canalmuseum.org
Artifacts, dioramas, working model of canal lock.

DeWint House (D)
Livingston St. and Oak Tree Rd.
Tappan, NY 10983
845-359-1359
Circa-1700 house was George Washington's HQ in American Revolution.

Dia:Beacon (G)
3 Beekman St.
Beacon, NY 12508
845-440-0100
www.diacenter.org
Former factory transformed into spectacular museum of modern art.

Donald M. Kendall Sculpture Garden (D)
700 Anderson Hill Rd.
Purchase, NY 10577
914-253-2000
Artwork arrayed around beautifully landscaped grounds.

Dutch Reformed Church (G)
125 Grand St.
Newburgh, NY 12551
www.newburghdrc.org
Imposing Greek Revival temple designed by noted 19th-century architect A.J. Davis.

Edward Hopper House (D)
82 North Broadway
Nyack, NY 10960
845-358-0774
www.edwardhopperhouseartcenter.org
Boyhood home of famed painter displays works by local artists.

**Eleanor Roosevelt National Historic Site
(Val-Kill)** (I)
Rte. 9G
Hyde Park, NY 12538
845-229-9115
www.nps.gov/elro
First Lady's unpretentious home.

FASNY American Museum of Firefighting (L)
117 Harry Howard Ave.
Hudson, NY 12534
518-822-8175
www.fasnyfiremuseum.com
Superb collection of fire trucks, hats, fire-fighting memorabilia.

Fort Montgomery State Historic Site (F)
815 Rte. 9W
Bear Mountain, NY 10911
845-786-2701, ext. 226
www.nysparks.state.ny.us/parks
Site of 1777 Revolutionary War battle; visitor center, intact redoubts.

Frances Lehman Loeb Art Center (H)
Vassar College
124 Raymond Ave.
Poughkeepsie, NY 12601
845-437-5632
www.fllac.vassar.edu
Collection ranges from antiquities to modern art; large display of Hudson River School paintings.

Hudson River Valley Heritage Area Sites – A Guide to the Region's Historic, Cultural, and Recreational Treasures

Letters in parentheses refer to location letters at top of map.

Franklin Delano Roosevelt National Historic Sites and Presidential Library (I)
4079 Albany Post Rd.
Hyde Park, NY 12538
1-800-FDR-VISIT
www.nps.gov/hofr
Roosevelt's lifelong home (Springwood); nation's first presidential library and museum; graves of FDR and Eleanor Roosevelt; Top Cottage, FDR's planned retirement home.

Fred J. Johnston Museum (J)
63 Main St.
Kingston, NY 12402
845-339-0720
www.fohk.org
Federal-style home with period furnishings.

Glebe House (H)
635 Main St.
Poughkeepsie, NY 12601
845-454-0605
Furnished Georgian-style home.

Gomez Mill House (H)
11 Mill House Rd.
Marlboro, NY 12542
845-236-3126
America's oldest extant Jewish residence, built 1714.

Harness Racing Museum & Hall of Fame (F)
240 Main St.
Goshen, NY 10924
845-294-6330
www.harnessmuseum.com
Paintings, trophies, other sporting memorabilia; virtual-reality ride recreates thrill of racing.

Hart-Cluett House (P)
57 Second St.
Troy, NY 12180
518-272-7232
www.rchsonline.org
Grand Federal-style townhouse; adjacent local-history museum.

Hill-Hold Museum (G)
Rte. 416
Campbell Hall, NY 10916
845-291-2404
Furnished 1769 stone farmhouse; outbuildings.

Hudson River Maritime Museum (J)
50 Rondout Landing
Kingston, NY 12401
845-338-0071
www.hrmm.org
Explores history of Hudson River commerce; boat trips to Rondout Lighthouse.

Hudson River Museum (C)
511 Warburton Ave.
Yonkers, NY 10701
914-963-4550
www.hrm.org
Changing exhibits on art, history; planetarium, restored Victorian mansion.

Hudson River Sloop Clearwater (H)
112 Little Market St.
Poughkeepsie, NY 12601
845-454-7673
www.clearwater.org
Educational sails aboard replica of 19th-century Hudson River sloop.

Huguenot Street Houses (I)
Huguenot Historical Society
18 Broadhead Ave.
New Paltz, NY 12561
845-255-1660
www.hhs-newpaltz.org
Seven circa-1700 stone houses of Huguenot settlers; reconstructed church.

Jacob Blauvelt House (E)
20 Zukor Rd.
New City, NY 10956
845-634-9629
www.rocklandhistory.org
19th-century Dutch farmhouse; adjacent museum of local history.

James Vanderpoel House (M)
16 Broad St., Rte. 9
Kinderhook, NY 12106
518-758-9265
www.cchsny.org
Superb Federal-style house; period furnishings.

Jasper Cropsey Studio & Gallery (C)
25 Cropsey Lane
Hastings-on-Hudson, NY 10706
914-478-7990
www.newingtoncropsey.com
Home of popular Hudson River School artist; extensive collection of his works.

John Jay Homestead State Historic Site (E)
400 Jay St. (Rte. 22)
Katonah, NY 10536
914-232-5651
www.nysparks.state.ny.us/parks
Home of first U.S. Supreme Court Chief Justice.

Katonah Museum of Art (E)
Rte. 22 at Jay St.
Katonah, NY 10536
914-232-9555
www.katonah-museum.org
Changing exhibits in architecturally notable building.

Knox's Headquarters State Historic Site (G)
Forge Hill Rd.
Vails Gate, NY 12584
845-561-5498
www.nysparks.state.ny.us/parks
HQ of Major General Henry Knox, Continental Army's commander of artillery.

Kykuit, the Rockefeller Estate (D)
Rte. 9
Sleepy Hollow, NY 10591
914-631-9491
www.hudsonvalley.org
Home to four generations of Rockefellers; outstanding gardens, sculpture collection.

Locust Grove, Samuel Morse Historic Site (H)
2683 South Rd.
Poughkeepsie, NY 12601
845-454-4500
www.morsehistoricsite.org
Tuscan-style villa of telegraph inventor and painter; walking trails, gardens.

Luykas Van Alen House (M)
Rte. 9H
Kinderhook, NY 12106
518-758-9265
www.cchsny.org
Outstanding 18th-century Dutch farmhouse.

Lyndhurst (D)
635 South Broadway
Tarrytown, NY 10591
914-631-4481
www.lyndhurst.org
Country's grandest Gothic Revival mansion.

Madam Brett Homestead (G)
50 Van Nydeck Ave.
Beacon, NY 12508
845-831-6533
Oldest house in Dutchess County, built 1709.

Manitoga: Russel Wright Design Center (F)
Rte. 9D
Garrison, NY 10524
845-424-3812
www.russelwrightcenter.org
Self-crafted home, studio, and grounds of influential 20th-century industrial designer.

Martin Van Buren National Historic Site (Lindenwald) (M)
1013 Old Post Rd.
Kinderhook, NY 12106
518-758-9689
www.nps.gov/mava
Elegant Italianate mansion was home of 14th U.S. President.

Hudson River Valley Heritage Area Sites — A Guide to the Region's Historic, Cultural, and Recreational Treasures

Letters in parentheses refer to location letters at top of map.

Montgomery Place (K)
1241 River Rd., Rte. 103
Annandale-on-Hudson, NY 12504
845-758-5461
www.hudsonvalley.org
Imposing Classical Revival mansion; grounds landscaped in 19th-century Romantic style.

Mount Gulian (G)
145 Sterling St.
Beacon, NY 12508
845-831-8172
www.mountgulian.org
Reconstructed headquarters of Friedrich von Steuben, Continental Army's drillmaster.

Museum of the Hudson Highlands (G)
25 Boulevard; also Rte. 9W
Cornwall, NY 12518
845-534-5506
www.museumhudsonhighlands.org
Science, nature exhibits; walking trails at Kenridge Farm (on Rte. 9W).

Neuberger Museum of Art (D)
735 Anderson Hill Rd.
Purchase, NY 10577
914-251-6100
www.neuberger.org
Excellent collection of contemporary American, African art.

New Windsor Cantonment State Historic Site (G)
374 Temple Hill Rd., Rte. 300
New Windsor, NY 12553
845-561-1765
www.nysparks.state.ny.us/parks
Final camp of Continental Army, 1782-3; also home to Purple Heart Hall of Honor.

New York State Capitol & Empire State Plaza Art Collection (O)
Albany, NY 12224
518-473-7521
One of America's grandest state capitols; large display of Abstract Expressionist paintings, sculpture.

New York State Museum (O)
Madison Ave.
Empire State Plaza
Albany, NY 12242
518-474-5877
www.nysm.nysed.gov
Explores natural, cultural history of state from age of dinosaurs to present.

Olana State Historic Site (L)
5720 Rte. 9G
Hudson, NY 12534
518-828-0135
www.nysparks.state.ny.us/parks
Persian-style villa of Hudson River School painter Frederic Edwin Church; house and grounds designed by artist.

Old Dutch Church (J)
272 Wall St.
Kingston, NY 12401
845-338-6759
www.olddutchchurch.org
Fascinating 19th-century church in Renaissance Revival style.

Old Rhinebeck Aerodrome (J)
Norton Rd.
P.O. Box 229
Rhinebeck, NY 12572
845-752-3200
www.oldrhinebeck.org
Museum of early aviation; air shows.

Opus 40 (K)
50 Fite Rd.
Saugerties, NY 12477
845-246-3400
www.opus40.org
Colossal environmental sculpture crafted in abandoned quarry.

Philipsburg Manor (D)
Rte. 9
Sleepy Hollow, NY 10591
914-631-8200
www.hudsonvalley.org
Explores role of enslaved Africans in valley's colonial development; working gristmill.

Philipse Manor Hall State Historic Site (C)
Warburton Ave. and Dock St.
Yonkers, NY 10702
914-965-4027
www.nysparks.state.ny.us/parks
Georgian-style home features some of country's finest Rococo ceilings.

Playland Amusement Park (C)
Playland Parkway
Rye, NY 10580
914-813-7000
www.ryeplayland.org
America's earliest planned amusement park; fascinating Art Deco architecture.

Poets' Walk Park (J)
River Rd. (County Rd. 103)
Annandale-on-Hudson, NY 12504
845-473-4440
www.scenichudson.org
Romantic landscape; breathtaking views of Hudson River, Catskills.

Putnam County Historical Society & Foundry School Museum (F)
63 Chestnut St.
Cold Spring, NY 10516
845-265-4010
www.pchsfsm.org
Exhibits on West Point Foundry, local history.

Richard B. Fisher Center (K)
Bard College
Annandale-on-Hudson, NY 12504
845-758-7900
www.bard.edu/fishercenter
Performing arts complex designed by Frank Gehry.

RiverSpark Visitor Center (P)
58 Remsen St.
Cohoes, NY 12047
518-237-7999
Sight-and-sound exhibit explores village's past as textile-manufacturing center.

Samuel Dorsky Museum of Art (SUNY New Paltz) (I)
75 South Manheim Blvd.
New Paltz, NY
845-257-3844
www.newpaltz.edu/museum
Changing art displays.

Saratoga National Historical Park (P)
648 Rte. 32
Stillwater, NY 12170
518-664-9821
www.nps.gov/sara
Site of 1777 battles deemed "turning point of the American Revolution."

Schuyler Mansion State Historic Site (O)
32 Catherine St.
Albany, NY 12202
518-434-0834
www.nysparks.state.ny.us/parks
Grand Georgian-style home of Philip Schuyler, colonial landowner/politician/general.

Senate House & Museum State Historic Site (J)
296 Fair St.
Kingston, NY 12401
845-338-2786
www.nysparks.state.ny.us/parks
Residence where state senate first convened (1777); museum features paintings, artifacts.

Hudson River Valley Heritage Area Sites – A Guide to the Region's Historic, Cultural, and Recreational Treasures

Letters in parentheses refer to location letters at top of map.

Shaker Museum & Library (N)
88 Shaker Museum Rd.
Old Chatham, NY 12136
518-794-9100
www.shakermuseumandlibrary.org
World's largest collection of furniture, other items crafted by religious sect.

Slabsides (I)
West Park, NY 12493
845-384-6320
Woodland retreat of author/naturalist John Burroughs.

St. Paul's Church National Historic Site (C)
897 South Columbus Ave.
Mount Vernon, NY 10550
914-667-4116
www.nps.gov/sapa
Restored 18th-century church.

Staatsburgh (Mills Mansion) State Historic Site (I)
Old Post Rd.
Staatsburg, NY 12580
845-889-8851
www.nysparks.state.ny.us/parks
Large Gilded Age mansion remodeled by architect Stanford White; expansive grounds.

Stone Barns Center for Food & Agriculture (D)
630 Bedford Rd.
Pocantico Hills, NY 10591
914-366-6200
www.stonebarnscenter.org
Housed in impressive Rockefeller barns; explores importance of local farming.

Stony Point Battlefield State Historic Site (E)
Park Rd.
Stony Point, NY 10980
845-786-2521
www.nysparks.state.ny.us/parks
British stronghold captured by Continental Army in 1779 raid; ruins of fortifications, museum, 19th-century lighthouse.

Storm King Art Center (F)
Old Pleasant Hill Rd.
Mountainville, NY 10953
845-534-3115
www.stormkingartcenter.org
Superb outdoor sculpture park; dramatic Hudson Highlands backdrop.

Sunnyside (D)
West Sunnyside Lane
Tarrytown, NY 10591
914-631-8200
www.hudsonvalley.org
Picturesque home of author Washington Irving; original furnishings.

Ten Broeck Mansion (O)
9 Ten Broeck Place
Albany, NY 12210
518-436-9826
Furnished Federal-style home.

Thomas Cole's Cedar Grove (L)
218 Spring St.
Catskill, NY 12414
518-943-7465
www.thomascole.org
Home and studio of founder of Hudson River School of Art.

Union Church of Pocantico Hills (D)
555 Bedford Rd.
Sleepy Hollow, NY 10591
845-631-8200
www.hudsonvalley.org
Brilliant stained glass windows by Marc Chagall and Henri Matisse.

U.S. Military Academy & Museum (F)
2107 South Post Rd.
West Point, NY 10996
845-938-2638
www.usma.edu
Incomparable collection of military memorabilia, paintings, weaponry.

U.S.S. Slater (O)
141 Broadway
Albany, NY 12201
518-431-1943
www.ussslater.org
Sole extant World War II destroyer escort in battle configuration.

Van Cortlandt Manor (E)
South Riverside Ave.
Croton-on-Hudson, NY 10520
914-631-8200
www.hudsonvalley.org
18th-century seat of one of valley's great landowning families.

Van Wyck Homestead Museum (G)
504 Rte. 9
Fishkill, NY 12524
845-896-9560
18th-century home, headquarters for important Revolutionary War supply depot.

Washington's Headquarters State Historic Site (G)
84 Liberty St.
Newburgh, NY 12551
845-562-1195
www.nysparks.state.ny.us/parks
Washington slept here longer than at any other Revolutionary War HQ; museum.

West Point Foundry Preserve (F)
Chestnut St.
Cold Spring, NY
845-473-4440
www.scenichudson.org
Ruins of 19th-century U.S. arsenal; produced Parrott guns credited with winning Civil War.

White Plains Battlefield (D)
Battle Ave. and Lincoln Ave.
White Plains, NY 10606
Site of 1776 battle from which Continental Army narrowly escaped defeat.

Wilderstein (J)
330 Morton Rd.
Rhinebeck, NY 12572
845-876-4818
www.wilderstein.org
Intact Queen Anne-style mansion; landscape by Central Park designer Calvert Vaux.

Fall

Preceding pages: Marist College crews glide through an autumn dawn reflected in the waters above Poughkeepsie.

Hudson Valley destinations include the October Antique Car Show at Mills Mansion, a state historic site in Staatsburg, and the great viewpoint on the grounds of Hyde Park's Vanderbilt Mansion National Historic Site.

Beautiful vistas are a Hudson Valley hallmark. The belvedere at Boscobel (above) looks onto the Hudson Highlands; New Jersey's Palisades loom across the river from the terrace within New York City's Wave Hill Park.

Preceding pages: Majestic View Farms at the foot of the Shawangunk Mountains.

The power of a painter's vision – Landscapes captured on canvas by Frederic Church from Olana, his Persian-style palace (above) near Hudson, have motivated a modern movement to protect his home's "viewshed."

Right: Within Olana's grounds, autumn brushstrokes embellish the shoreline of the lake he designed.

A bountiful valley – Montgomery Place Orchards offers 60 apple varieties; pumpkins await pickers in frost-kissed fields.

Washington Irving's "The Legend of Sleepy Hollow" inspires living hysteria at Historic Hudson Valley sites. The Great Jack O'Lantern Blaze at Van Cortlandt Manor attracts thousands of fright-seekers. Legend Weekend at Philipsburg Manor stars a chorus of ghouls, goblins, and – of course – a headless horseman.

Day's end at Rockwood Hall State Park (right) on the Hudson's Tappan Zee; season's end at Fahnestock State Park in the Hudson Highlands.

Overleaf: River's end at the Statue of Liberty in New York Harbor.